ABLE TO BE
OTHERWISE

A MEMOIR

ABLE TO BE OTHERWISE

A MEMOIR

ANNA LENAKER

NEW DEGREE PRESS
COPYRIGHT © 2021 ANNA LENAKER

ABLE TO BE OTHERWISE
A Memoir

ISBN   978-1-63676-719-2 *Paperback*
            978-1-63730-048-0 *Kindle Ebook*
            978-1-63730-150-0 *Ebook*

Table of Contents

The answer must be, I think, that beauty and grace are performed whether or not we will or sense them. The least we can do is try to be there.

—ANNIE DILLARD, *Pilgrim at Tinker Creek*

This book is dedicated to my mom and to the town of Paradise, California, that was razed to the ground by the Camp Fire in 2018.

Author's Note

This book is a record of my breaths.

Imagine my shock and disbelief when I—a first-generation, low-income student with no parents—received a full ride to attend Brown University. Surprise held my breath captive long after I read that magic word: "Congratulations."

My first semester at Brown, I learned how to breathe again. I participated in workshops led by the contemplative studies department faculty that taught me how to control my breath and exist in the present moment. It's much harder than it sounds.

It went a little bit like this . . .

I slowly breathe in, relishing the sunbeams pouring through the window, warming me to the core. As I inhale deep breaths, my eyelids droop low, letting in only the faintest hints of shapes and colors. My ears are ever more alert in the still room of breathers. The quiet offers me the opportunity to hear things that often go unheard: the rustling of the leaves outside, the creaking of branches flexing in the breeze, and my own breath. Exhale.

I notice the clamping down of my jaw, my raised shoulders, and my more rapid, shallow breaths when a memory takes advantage of my mind's stillness. I picture my memories as books, occupying rows and rows of cranial bookshelves. Some sport a fine layer of dust, some unfortunately lie entirely forgotten on shelves in dimly lit corners of my mind's library, and others are worn from their constant summoning. This last category enters during moments of stillness: those painful memories that refuse to be unwritten. Their familiar tear-stained pages still manage to force the breath from my lungs.

I visualize a healing touch undoing the chains that tether my trauma to my body. Inhale. As my mind wanders through scenes of grief and hardship, I gently lead it back to the present. It is time to heal, to decide how I want to spend the time I've been allotted to help heal others and alleviate a bit of the suffering around me. Each time I breathe deeply, I become a little lighter, a little more present. Exhale.

This book explores the moments in time, now memories, when my breaths have come quicker, shallower, have all but stopped, and meandered peacefully in and out of my lungs. I will share with you my memories of breaths that have survived poverty, despaired over addiction's stranglehold on a loved one, and gasped as they witnessed the horrors of climate change. I will also share with you my memories of breaths that have proclaimed joy and love in the midst of heartache.

This book is also an experiment in imagining how the way we as a society think about and approach our greatest problems could be otherwise. It resists the despair and resignation that I and so many of us feel when faced with problems as immense as poverty, addiction, and climate change.

I share these memories of both my lightest and most labored breaths as a small contribution toward the larger ongoing effort of breathing a more gentle, more compassionate future into existence. Just as we are healed slowly through the succession of our breaths, we must use our breaths to protect and heal others. Let us take it even further and use our breaths to heal and protect our Earth.

The first step toward healing is to breathe. Inhale. Breath is the anchor that grounds us in this strange reality where we all exist on a rock spinning in a vacuum. This is where the second step comes in. Wondering and marveling at the world and its happenings aids our healing. Beholding the beautiful, improbable, and incredible expands our reasons for living. As I wonder at the improbability of my loved ones' and my existence on this planet, I am grateful and joyous. I am healing.

Breath is another way to think about time. Like the second or minute, breath is a marker of continuity. With time comes healing. To get through grief, you just get through it. Be patient with yourself. As your breaths follow one after the other, you are healing. Like a tree slowly growing out of the scorched earth after a fire, healing will follow loss. Breathe in. Breathe out.

It is through the breaths of protestors and the breaths of those demanding to be seen and heard that we are breathing a future into existence that values all of our breaths and values everyone's healing. It will take many breaths, but there are a lot of us.

Inhale. Let a deep breath fill up your lungs. Feel your body become lighter; feel your mind become more focused on the present. Let the oxygen energize you. Do you feel your power?

Each time we dare to acknowledge that things are able to be otherwise, we move toward a world where everyone can breathe deeper.

Introduction

———

I am engulfed by a symphony of crickets, their chirps made ever louder by the depth of the darkness that surrounds me. My classmates and I are out for a silent night walk in a small patch of woods a mile away from Brown University's campus in Providence, Rhode Island. We are trying to walk silently with intention and attention, to sense our surroundings, and to focus on all of the muscles and movements that make up the act of walking. I let myself appreciate the swinging of my legs, slowing myself to match the rhythm of the shadow I can just barely make out in front of me. I focus on calming my breathing into a steady rhythm that mirrors the movements of my limbs.

We head in no specific direction. Our professor called us to these woods on a field trip to see what we might learn from them and from each other as we enjoy a contemplative walk together. Although we started out as a cohesive group of twenty, we soon fracture into subgroups as we lose each other in the darkness. A few others and I manage to head off down a leaf-slick slope, a rather sharp detour from the well-worn path above.

Slipping and sliding down the slope, we grab onto the rough bark of small trees to halt our descent. Realizing we are lost in the dark of this city-bound forest, we erupt into laughter.

At first, I try to stifle my laughter, worried it may be inappropriate given our vow of silence. But it bursts forth nonetheless, drowning out the chirping of the crickets. I picture our laughter as a joyful offering to the woods in recognition of the limits of our sight and the shortness of our lives.

To laugh is to be firmly rooted in the present, just as to focus on one's breath is to be intensely aware of one's existence. To laugh with others is to celebrate the pleasure of each other's company and, at times, a way of mutually recognizing the absurdity of a shared condition.

When our bellies hurt from straining muscles and our lungs hurt from expelling air, we slowly amble back up the slope in search of our classmates. We circle together in a wide clearing to share our experiences and thoughts. Looking back, this is one of my favorite college experiences.

I like to think of this night in the woods as an apt metaphor for navigating uncertainty and suffering in this life. Regarding uncertainty, I'm learning to accept that life resists being planned. It is not possible to see all the steps ahead of us when the future resists being beholden. In the moments when we find ourselves off of the path we predicted lay ahead, community becomes a vital resource. We laugh, celebrate, mourn, learn, and comfort in communities. It is in community that we are re-energized, and it is together that we find our way back to the path.

Or consider this: suffering is a thick blanket of darkness that surrounds us on all sides at times. With suffering so all-consuming, it can be hard to trudge onward, and it can be easy to get lost. We all suffer in different ways and at different times. This is unavoidable. What's important, though, is that we are there alongside those who are also suffering, providing company, encouragement, and understanding. It is important that we have people in our lives who are there alongside us when suffering takes its grip. Community is a buoyant force. In community, we can be lifted from the deepest pits of despair. This power that community has, though, is only possible when we agree to be lifted and we agree to lift up others.

These times seem particularly heavy with uncertainty and suffering. This book is very much a reaction to all that we have experienced together during this prolonged quarantine. Hundreds of thousands of lives have been claimed by a pandemic that has driven countless individuals deeper into poverty, addiction, and despair. Income inequality continues to grow as the rich become richer, while tens of millions of people around the globe have fallen into poverty as a result of the pandemic.[1] The opioid epidemic continues to claim lives as individuals find themselves lonely and without the medical resources they need. Wildfires of historic proportions have burned up and down the West Coast. And, for the first time in a long time, I have found myself with time to reflect.

I graduated with a master's degree in public affairs from Brown University at my family's dining room table in the spring of 2020. I had no future plans and

---

1   Christoph Lakner et al., "Updated Estimates of the Impact of COVID-19 on Global Poverty: Looking Back at 2020 and the Outlook for 2021," *World Bank Blogs*, January 11, 2021.

was very distressed over the magnitude of our collective challenges. Confined in our rural Northern California home, I knew I had to do something to help heal a world in pain, a world grieving over loss of life and injustice. As poverty, addiction, and climate change became common issues discussed alongside COVID-19, I saw an opportunity to contribute to these conversations.

This book is a testament to my belief in the power of stories to provide comfort, to aid in understanding, to delight and inspire, and even to change minds. I share my story with the hope of bringing increased compassion and understanding to conversations surrounding poverty, addiction, and climate change.

This book is also a celebration of the power of community and of hopeful imagining. With every loss and every injustice, there is a community of people who are grieving, comforting, and demanding that such suffering never happen again. I write this book in recognition of the many people who have cared about me and brought me into their communities. This book dares its reader to believe that together we are able to transform the imagined into reality so long as we take the first step: believing that things are able to be otherwise. We must labor and breathe and laugh together. We must support each other and be kind to one another.

My hope is that you walk away from this book empowered to imagine alternatives and with the conviction that things are able to be other than the way they are. This world is a work in progress waiting to be transformed by our collective imagination. As I join many others in this exercise of hopeful imagining, I hope you'll join me too.

Mom decided, after hearing the voice of God, that we were intended to pack up our lives in Murrieta Hot Springs, California, and head south for the border. I was just turning seven years old, and we were moving to Tijuana, Mexico, where she had been told she was to meet the love of her life. The love of her life turned out to be named Alex. A yellow taxi driver, Alex was convinced that he, too, had met the love of his life in my mom.

Mom had woken me up late one night to break the news. Lying beside me on the bed, she stroked my forehead until I managed to partially crack open my eyes. Her permed brown curls framed her face alight with revelation.

"Susie, Susie, wake up!" she whispered excitedly. "We're moving to Tijuana."

"What? Why? Where is that?" My questions blended in with each other. My confusion shocked me fully awake as my eyes searched Mom's face for the reason behind this altogether unexpected announcement.

"I've been going down to Tijuana the last few weekends," she explained. "When you were with your sitter, I was following the voice of God. God told me to go down to Tijuana last month in church, I heard Him, and I listened. Minutes after I crossed the border that first time, I met him."

"Him?" *Is she saying she met God in the flesh?*

"I met Alex. I know we just met, but I love him. God led me to him, and we are going to move to Mexico to stay with him," she declared.

I never asked what specifically God had told her in church. I figured it had to be pretty convincing to get Mom to pack up our lives and pull me out of school. Mom was happy for what seemed like the first time in a long time, so I went along with it. I wanted her to be happy.

In the years before Mexico, we lived in a two-story apartment along a quiet street. The front yard of our apartment was an endless land to be explored. Populated by mysterious trees bearing berries, ladybugs, bushes, rocks, and discarded toys, I spent many of my young days getting to know the terrain and its inhabitants. I never grew tired of my expeditions, and the yard was, in my mind, vast and inexhaustible. The small alleyway that snaked along the far and backside of the apartment complex was the secret trail I took to surprise my friends when we played tag. It allowed me to pass undetected from one side of the complex to another.

While I can't recall my first memory, I do have a distinct first love. When not outdoors, my young years were spent in front of the television watching the original *Scooby-Doo* episodes on VHS. I idolized the friendship between Scooby and Shaggy, the way Fred lays out a perfect plan although it is never executed perfectly, and the way Velma seems to either have all the answers or at least know how to find them. Life for the Scooby gang was never boring.

I watched *Scooby-Doo* amid piles of Mom's books (a good share of them being vampire romance novels), clothing, and random trinkets. My mom was a hoarder, but I was too young to know of the existence of any other way of living. Child Protective Services intervened when I was a handful of years old, telling my mom that if the house wasn't cleaned up, she was going to be deemed unfit to parent. Apparently, the piles upon piles of stuff, dirty dishes, and our daily habits meant that my home environment was not safe for me. Family pitched in to help, and soon the place was tidier.

"When the CPS people come to our house tomorrow," Mom told me, "it's important that they see you are happy and healthy here."

"Okay, what if they don't think that?" I could see the stress in Mom's eyes. I knew she wasn't telling me something. Anxiously, I clutched my favorite stuffed bear, Girl, closer to my chest.

"You need to convince them, okay? So you can stay here with me."

"I want to stay here with you. Please don't let them take me." I was beginning to panic. I could feel my heart beating in my neck.

"It'll turn out all right. Just smile and answer their questions," Mom spoke softly as she stroked my hair back from my forehead.

The next morning, I sat on the couch and smiled at strangers as they roamed around our house. When asked about my quality of life, I assured them I couldn't be any happier. Our house remained clean for about a month after the inspection. While we could put on a show for CPS, actual change was hard to come by.

Some months after the CPS fiasco, my mom took me to an adoption agency. When we first pulled up to the building, I squinted at the sign in confusion, but Mom did not offer up any explanation to relax my furrowed brow. I spent the next hour wandering around and playing with some of the kids while Mom talked to some administrative personnel. All that time I was paralyzed with fear that she was trying to leave me there, to confirm for herself that it was a nicer place for me to grow up. I wondered if she had started to believe that CPS was right to be concerned about my living with her.

"Were you thinking about . . . Were you going to . . ." I babbled in incomplete sentences as we pulled away from the agency, trying to think of the best way to ask whether she had been thinking about leaving me behind.

"What?"

"Nothing. Never mind." If the answer was "yes," I didn't want to know it. I would not be able to bear it.

Once we were on the freeway speeding away from the adoption agency, I exhaled a sigh of relief. I still feel that sigh of relief reverberate through my body each time I am accepted by a loved one, each time there is an unspoken invitation to stay.

I believe that people are too complex to be labeled "good" or "bad." We hear of good parents and bad parents, but I've never been able to label mine. I never met my dad. When Mom found out she was pregnant, she left late in the night without telling him. My older half-brother, Jay, told me my dad's name when I was thirteen years old. We had been driving for hours, desert hills and power lines rushing by us, when it suddenly occurred to me that I didn't know my father's name.

"Martin," he told me. I googled it, found nothing, and that's been the end of that search.

Mom tried her best to provide for me as a single mother. Though she ran away from home and dropped out of high school after the tenth grade despite being a straight-A student, she studied independently years later and got her GED. When she had money, she'd get me a gift, or my favorite popsicles, or take me to get my favorite meal: fries and ketchup. She tried really hard to be there for me despite her struggles and demons. Part of me thinks she never had a chance to be the typical "good" mom. She scraped by financially, struggled with mental health problems her entire life, and bounced from abusive relationship to abusive relationship.

Jay tells me that many of the men Mom dated were physically and emotionally abusive, dangerous, and vile men. They were violent by nature and even more violent when drunk; take Derek, for example. Derek was a radio DJ for a Colorado rock station, a black belt, and an avid partier. When drunk, he'd like to get into fights and pick on people. Mom wouldn't let him pick on her, but when she stood up to him and punched him in the face, she ended up in the hospital. Jay recalls the cops being called multiple times over the course of one year to break up domestic fights between Mom and her suitors.

Mom struggled throughout her life to be happy in simple, loving relationships, Jay tells me. She never seemed to be happy with the "nice guy"—not with the Filipino sailor who wanted to show her the world or the Colorado used car salesmen who took her dancing. By the time I was born, Mom had decided to be single for a while. I struggle to imagine what it would have been like for Jay to grow up with strange, scary men around. I imagine that there is no sense of home when all you come back to is violence and meanness. Despite the turmoil, Jay recalls never doubting that he was loved by Mom or that, underneath the grittiness of her circumstances, she had a warm heart.

Mom's path was certainly not an easy one to walk. Once her mother died just a few years before I was born, I'm told that she was never quite herself again. Once Mom was sucked into the current of grief, she never resurfaced. Pictures of Mom's mother hung upon our fridge until the day we moved to Tijuana. Mom always told me how wonderful her mom was and how she wished that I had gotten the chance to meet her. I do wish I had been able to meet my grandmother. I still long for those homemade sweaters and knitted blankets, those words of wisdom that only come with decades of lived experience.

Seventeen years my senior, Jay was the one who took care of me when Mom was at work. He would lug me in his arms to his band practices and gigs, setting me down by the kick drum. Hypnotized by his rhythm and graceful movements, I'd watch as he performed complex, rehearsed patterns that involved pressing down the kick drum pedal, lightly tapping the hi-hat, thumping the snare drum and toms, and whacking various cymbals that hung suspended at the peak of his drum set.

"My brother is a rock star," I'd later tell my young friends, who would "ooh" in appreciation.

When playing the drums, Jay always had the most concentrated of expressions, his head of spiked hair bobbing up and down with the tide of his rhythm as waves of vibrations emanated out to the audience. Listening to him play his drums was as soothing to me as the bouncing chair he placed me in before I could walk.

When Mom wasn't home, Jay would feed me brownies and let me jump on the bed. Once Mom found out, we certainly got in trouble, but no amount of scolding could change the fact that we were junk food eaters. Chocolate and sweets of all sorts filled our house when Jay was around. Jay even made a hilarious home video that was a compilation of close-up shots of our overweight cat Baby and our countertops filled with a variety of Hostess treats, chips, chocolate, and more. Baby, the video suggested, was going a bit overboard with the snacking and was the perfect scapegoat for our feasting.

Jay was a drummer for a local Christian youth group band. They were so good they got to tour around Europe playing at different venues, including a parliamentary building in Brussels. Jay still fondly recalls the delicious waffles he had in Belgium on that trip and the stunning architecture of Brussels' downtown square. For Jay, church was a haven, a place to escape the hardships and find community. It's where he met his now wife of eighteen years, my sister-in-law, Teressa. It's where he found a home away from our tumultuous homelife.

Jay moved out when I was about five years old, but he still visited often. He and Teressa lived but a mile or so away in a condo they bought right after their wedding. At their wedding, I was their flower girl dressed in blue and sparkles. I had walked down the aisle sprinkling petals while clutching Girl in the crook of my arm. I never went anywhere without Girl. Girl was named by Mom and Jay because I had a hard time pronouncing the hard "r" sound; it always came out as a sort of "w." Instead of getting me a speech therapist, they named the object I treasured most in the world with a name that forced me to practice my pronunciation. They'd grill me constantly on it. To this day, I have to think pretty intentionally about forming the hard "r" sound, but I can do it. What a brilliant, cost-effective plan they had! It really worked.

Teressa was a warm, stabilizing force. She was the one who had helped Mom clean up the house before CPS came to do its inspection. I could tell that she cared deeply for my brother and me. I don't remember first meeting Teressa. Her coming into my life was so seamless and natural that it felt as if she had always been a part of the family, her smile always a part of my day.

While Mom never told me that we were poor, it was clear to me that money was tighter for us than it was for others. I didn't have many toys beyond my beloved Scooby-Doo Mystery Machine, my marbles, my books, my bike, and some puzzles. When I went over to friends' houses, their rooms were filled with dolls, action figures, race cars and tracks, sports equipment, and more. My friends would ask me what I wanted to play with, and I wouldn't know where to start. I would be overwhelmed by the options. Even though others had more, I was, for the most part, very satisfied with what I did have. I knew Mom had worked hard to get me what I had.

There were times when food was scarcer than was comfortable. Mom and I would drive to a local food bank and pick up a paper bag filled with groceries. If the food bank's stock was depleted or we needed more groceries, she'd drive us around to local churches. We'd knock on their doors and Mom would ask if they had any groceries they could donate. Most did not have a food pantry, but a handful of pastors were kind enough to give Mom some money to buy us food for a couple of days. I was always shocked by this kindness given to complete strangers.

I personally hated asking for help. I would shrink behind Mom during these encounters, peering at pastors from behind the folds of her clothes. Mom had suggested my asking might be more effective at getting support. I tried a couple of times but didn't feel comfortable doing so. I didn't like to admit that we were struggling; admitting that we were short of food felt like a weakness.

It is only now that I know I was one of millions of children who lived in food-insecure households in the United States. In 2019, it was estimated by the USDA that over 13 percent of children in the United States live in households that are food insecure.[2] While some of these households receive government benefits, like SNAP (food stamps) and/or WIC, the benefit levels are not always sufficient to cover a family's full nutritional needs. Feeding America, a national network of food banks that serves tens of millions, reports that over 40 percent of the people they assist also receive SNAP benefits.[3] As Mom knew, food banks, religious organizations, and other community organizations often fill the gaps between governmental support and a low-income family's nutritional needs.

Our food insecurity was just one manifestation of the reality that we lived paycheck to paycheck for my whole childhood. We'd walk through stores adding up the value of everything we placed in our cart. I got very good at mental math. Each time Mom added something to the cart, I'd give her the updated count of where we were at, even factoring in the tax. Years down the road, I became recognized as my sixth-grade class' mental-math whiz—a triumph I owe to these early experiences of being broke.

Again, it is only now that I know we were one of the many families that live paycheck to paycheck. A 2019 survey of American adults found that 49 percent expected to live paycheck to paycheck in 2020—a percentage that has no doubt increased since the onset of the pandemic.[4] Many of these workers—nearly 30

---

2 "Key Statistics & Graphics," United States Department of Agriculture Economic Research Service. September 9, 2020.

3 "SNAP-Eligible Households," Feeding America. Accessed February 28, 2021.

4 "Study: 53% of US Adults Don't Have Emergency Fund," First National Bank of Omaha press release, February 19, 2020.

percent of Americans—have no emergency savings.[5] Nearly 100 million Americans are one emergency away from having no money to their names. With so much uncertainty in life, this is a scary reality.

Before our move to Tijuana, Mom worked the graveyard shift at the county jail to try to make ends meet. Before work, she'd prepare a thermos with her preferred cocktail: a screwdriver, composed of orange juice and a generous pour of vodka. I didn't fully understand what vodka was, but I knew that it made work more bearable. Mom was able to do a job she hated when she had her thermos with her. It was the same thermos that she drank from on her days off, late at night after she had put me to bed, when she was rewatching one of the few movies she seemed to always watch.

"These aren't kid movies," she'd remind me when I would visit the living room late at night in search of permission to stay up late and watch *The Silence of the Lambs* with her. If I were standing close enough, I would be able to smell the contents of her thermos on her breath.

"Alright," I'd grumble as I huffed my way back up the stairs. "Someday," I'd mutter to myself.

While I wasn't invited to watch late-night movies with Mom, I was encouraged to go to church with her. In the year before Tijuana, we regularly attended a local Pentecostal church. Mom always emerged from the service with a temporary glow. Her smile was always a bit wider afterward. I remember waiting in line with Mom to approach the pastor. When her turn came, the

---

5   Amanda Dixon, "A Growing Percentage of Americans Have No Emergency Savings Whatsoever," Bankrate. July 1, 2019.

pastor and other members of the congregation would lay hands on her and shout prayers in languages foreign to me. If I listened close enough, I could make out English phrases thrown into the mix: "sister in Christ," "in need of healing," "grief's tight grip," "reminded of your love," "let there be…no more pain."

The praying would crescendo, voices layering upon one another, until she collapsed on the stage alongside those who had gone up before her. Her limp body would be caught by a volunteer that gently lowered her to the ground alongside the other collapsed bodies. "Hallelujah!" spectators would sing out.

It was during one of these experiences that Mom heard from God. Sometimes she'd have me come all the way up to the stage with her, and when it was time to collapse, I fell along with her, praying that the volunteer would catch me. While I didn't enjoy the risk of falling and smacking my head on the carpeted wooden stage, it was important to Mom, and, as with many things, I was willing to go along with it.

I was but a few weeks into second grade when Mom pulled me out of school. There had been a closed-door meeting where Mom explained to the administrators that I would be continuing my education abroad. I sat outside on a sun-faded but still distinctly blue plastic chair listening intently to the conversation through the wall. What exactly my education abroad would look like was not expanded upon. I was not happy about the absence of a definitive plan for getting me back into school. I loved going to school, playing my teachers at checkers, and learning my way through the stacks of books in the library. Would there be a library in Tijuana, I wondered? And if there was, would there be any books in English? I tried my best to not think about these unknowns. I was, after all, powerless to do anything about them. I shifted my attention instead to my upcoming seventh birthday.

I had a co-birthday party with my friend next door, Angelique, the day before Mom's and my move to Tijuana. We had a bounce house and a Scooby-Doo and SpongeBob-themed cake. I was over the moon with excitement the entire day. I practically lived in the bounce house for the eight hours that we had rented it. When my legs could bounce no more, I laid down, enjoying the feeling of the inflated ridges holding me up. Mom had to deflate the bounce house with me still inside. It was only when Mom started folding it up that I crawled my way out onto the grass.

Angelique and I decided to head down to the public pool to celebrate the last evening of our friendship. We both knew we probably weren't going to see each other again, but neither of us dared speak this reality out loud. Knowing nothing about the mechanics of swimming, we clung to our foam noodles and tiptoed in. Enjoying the cool water, we became overly confident in the ability of a single foam noodle to ensure our safety as we progressed into the deepest section of the pool. We gazed upwards at the clouds passing overhead.

"A pirate ship! Do you see it?" I exclaimed, nudging Angelique with my elbow.

"Looks more like a dragon to me. See the wings there, the fire being breathed out there," she instructed, pointing up at the sky.

I had barely looked away in search of other clouds when there was a commotion of splashing and the frightening sensation of my noodle being ripped out from under my arms. Angelique had lost hold of her own noodle and claimed mine.

My head plunged below the surface of the water.

Opening my mouth to yell for help, I only ended up sucking in mouthfuls of chlorinated water. Inhale. I heard the gurgling sound of water rushing into my mouth, silencing my yells. I thrashed about, struggling to reach the surface, struggling to learn how to swim through sheer willpower, but I was drowning. I couldn't command my terror-stricken body to relax or my mouth to shut.

I was slowly surrendering to the pool's depths, my senses growing dimmer as I processed my shock at my unexpected demise. I slid my eyes shut.

My friend's mom had sprinted from her chair at the other end of the pool area and jumped in to rescue me. I came to, lying on the dirty concrete that ringed the pool, spitting up water and gasping for oxygen. Angelique's mom's face hovered just above my own.

"I'm alive. I'm fine," I muttered, noticing the chemical rawness of my throat and the way my whole body felt heavy.

I sat in utter silence during the drive home, barely making eye contact with Angelique. I was in shock. Angelique had been shocked, too, shivering on the concrete, coughing. Her mom had pulled her out first, then come back for me. I couldn't tell if I was mad at Angelique for yanking my noodle from me. I eventually decided I wasn't. People do what they need to do to survive. I would come to learn this on the streets of Tijuana. In hindsight, my near drowning feels like it was an omen for our struggles to come. It was my first lesson in how thrilling it is to be alive after going through an ordeal.

I arrived home, my hair a damp, tangled mop, my voice hoarse as I explained to Mom what had happened.

Mom's eyes were panicked. "You're okay. You're okay," she murmured as she rhythmically patted my back. "You don't have to do anymore packing. I'll handle it. You can just watch Scooby and have some more of your cake."

She stationed me on the ground in front of the TV with a plateful of cake. The furniture had been stripped from the room, and only half-filled boxes and random magazines, books, clothing, and knickknacks littered the floor. As my shock from drowning ebbed, it was replaced with worry as the hours before our move ticked down. I thought of Jay and Teressa, my only other family. When would I see them again? I knew Jay wasn't thrilled about Mom moving me to Mexico, but there was no dissuading her. I watched Scooby and Shaggy flee from what appeared to be a re-animated mummy. No matter how dicey things seemed to get, Scooby and Shaggy always managed to not only make it out all right but to triumph over that which they feared. Panic was part of their method. I decided to let myself be a little panicked and a bit worried.

I woke up the next morning to all of our belongings stuffed into the back of a U-Haul. We were leaving all of our furniture behind and bringing only our favorite possessions with us for our new life on the other side of the border. Just over an hour's drive from the border crossing into Tijuana, we became one of many cars, trucks, and motorcycles lined up single file across a dozen queues, waiting their turn to officially cross into Mexico.

Vendors selling freshly made churros, roasted corn, and trinkets weaved around cars, yelling out their product descriptions to their captive audience. To this day, the border churros are the best I've had. The perfect blend of sugar, cinnamon, and oil crisped and coated the spiraling dough, providing comfort to those who had grown restless of the wait. We pulled ahead car by car. Mom was eager to start building her new life with Alex. I was nervous and unsure. I had yet to meet Alex, I'd never left the country before, I didn't speak Spanish, and I was supposed to be in school. Mom continued to assure me that all would work out and that Alex was "the one," a great guy, a guy approved by God himself.

When we finally made it to the front of our line, Mom hand-cranked the wide window of the U-Haul down and peered at the border crossing inspector, answering his questions as to what exactly we were up to moving to Mexico alone, knowing no Spanish. Once Mom convinced the inspector that we were as serious as could be, that she was on a divinely sanctioned mission to uproot our lives and start afresh, she was told to unlock the back of the truck for them to conduct an examination of its contents.

Instructed to wait in the vehicle, we sat quietly in the truck for a half hour, nervous about the inspector's final word on the viability of our plan. Once the inspection was complete, we were informed that they had removed a few "prohibited" items from our belongings and that we were good to pull forward into Tijuana. Not knowing what they took, we bowed to the pressure of those anxiously waiting behind us and drove on. It was only later that I discovered that they had taken many of my toys. I realized that "prohibited" was a label they used to justify robbery.

Just after we'd officially crossed the border into Tijuana, we were on a highway littered with billboards and advertisements guiding us toward the yellow taxi hub. There we found Alex waiting for us. He was dressed in crisp black slacks, shined black shoes, and a soft yellow long-sleeved shirt tucked in and secured with a black leather belt. This was the outfit he wore each day for years on end. His short hair was jet black, just like his mustache; he smelled of a strong cologne that became even stronger when he embraced me for a hug.

"*Hola*," I said, using my first word of Spanish that Mom taught me during our drive down.

"*Hola, chiquita*," he responded with a soft smile. Mom and Alex embraced, and I noticed Mom smiling wide, just like she did after we left church. I began to sense that maybe this really would be a new start for us.

Piling into the U-Haul, Alex drove us to our new home but twenty minutes away from the border. Alex was the first man that Mom introduced me to and the first one that I would be living with. As we drove to our new home, I wondered if Alex would ever feel like a father to me. I wondered what it even felt like to have a father. My musings were cut short by our arrival at a two-story yellow house that was near the exact shade of Alex's shirt. Surrounded by a wall of concrete bricks interlocked with steel rebar, the house sat right across the street from that of Alex's family. His mom, sisters, brothers, and cousins waved to us as we arrived.

Entering the house, I was struck by its emptiness. A single chair occupied the living room along with a TV that sat atop a milk crate. The chair was surrounded by an army of empty beer bottles. Their patterned arrangement gave off the impression that they were advancing toward an unseen threat. If someone kicked one over, it would no doubt set off a chain reaction of emptied Coronas tumbling into each other like dominoes. Alex, it seemed, shared Mom's affinity for alcohol.

My room was up the tiled stairs. I furnished it with a small bed, along with a small TV, VHS player, and the toys I had left. Alex got me some workbooks that introduced the basics of Spanish. I eagerly worked through them, missing the worksheets I had been given in school. Alex introduced me to his family, and I immediately tried out some of the vocabulary I had learned from the workbooks. They smiled and sat me down for my first Tijuana breakfast.

On my own, I tried to learn soccer from the local kids playing in the street right outside our house and explored the neighborhood. There was a corner store selling fresh tortillas daily a stone's throw away, as well as massive bags of rice and beans. I'd occasionally make runs to pick up ingredients for our dinner with Alex's family; I'd practically beg for the honor. I loved the smell of fresh corn tortillas and enjoyed the feeling of responsibility.

I spent much of my time at Alex's family's house. Alex slept well into the day after working night shifts at the taxi hub, and Mom either slept with him or went out and about on her own. Alex's sister taught me a few phrases in Spanish, and for my further edification, she parked me in front of the TV to watch *SpongeBob SquarePants* in Spanish, hoping I'd absorb additional vocabulary through deep immersion in Bikini Bottom. While Alex and two of his other siblings spoke a decent amount of English, the rest of his family spoke little. We communicated, instead, through facial expressions and lots of pointing. Alex's mom—Abuelita, I called her—taught me to mop and to sort out bad pinto beans from the good, as well as how to make traditional Mexican rice.

I enjoyed helping out around the kitchen and keeping the house clean, as I had never had the privilege of doing so before. In the States, Mom did not cook much, and rarely was our house uncluttered enough to even worry about cleaning the floor. I loved spending time with Alex's family and did not mind the language barrier; just their presence was enough. I spent many an afternoon watching telenovelas with Abuelita, watching her as she crocheted and delighted in the drama on-screen. I was thankful to have a family large enough to fill a dinner table and happy enough to eat together. Mom and I had never sat at the dinner table just the two of us. It had felt too empty.

In Mexico, Mom and I had the promise of a new and more full life. For Mom, Mexico was a promised land, a place where she hoped the worries and the struggles of her past would lose their grip and get caught up at the border. Mexico was the place where she felt she would finally get the life she deserved.

But after our first month in Tijuana, we ran out of money.

Mom had no desire for formal employment. She had hated her job at the jail in the US and didn't want to return to a similar misery. She was looking for an escape from reality: a place where she could exist and be loved and have all that she needed. Alex began to give Mom a stipend to buy the basics we needed, like food and clothing. Our stipend, however, was rapidly eaten up during our night drives when Mom would go out and buy her supply.

My mom was one of the early victims of the opioid epidemic. In the 1990s, doctors increasingly prescribed opioids to patients for pain relief after being assured by pharmaceutical companies that they were not addictive. Previously, opioid prescriptions had been reserved for those experiencing severe pain, post-surgical pain, or cancer patients receiving end-of-life care.[6] But as any form of pain became an increasing focus of the medical profession as something curable and as new pills were marketed aggressively as non-addictive pain relievers, doctors prescribed opioids at an increasing rate to patients.[7]

Mom first discovered opioids when she had a terrible case of kidney stones. I was around five years old then. Mom had woken me up with her screams. I ran to her side, watching in horror as she doubled over in agony, clutching her sides. At the hospital, she laid in a white gown, her eyes tired, as she assured me over and over again that she was in fact not dying but had sharp little rocks inside of her. I imagined them by the dozens, tearing up her insides, and collapsed in a chair by her side, listening to the buzz of the sterile fluorescent lights overhead, letting my eyes blur with tears until all I could make out was white: white light, white walls, white gown, white floor.

Mom and I went home early the next morning with a bottle of pills. Though Mom's first use of opioids was

6   Gery P. Guy et al., "Vital Signs: Changes in Opioid Prescribing in the United States, 2006-2015," *Morbidity and Mortality Weekly Report* 66, no. 26 (July 7, 2017): 697-704.

7   Jonathan K. Phillips, Morgan A. Ford, and Richard J. Bonnie, eds. "Pain Management and the Opioid Epidemic: Balancing Societal and Individual Benefits and Risks of Prescription Opioid Use." *PubMed.* National Academies Press (July 13, 2017): 187.

medicinal, it slowly morphed into recreational. Mom got more pills long after her kidney stones had passed.

Between 1999 and 2011, the number of opioid prescriptions in the US continued to rise each year, with the use of certain types increasing more than fivefold.[8] Alongside increasing prescription rates, the strength of the prescribed opioids continued to rise. Given that individuals were prescribed opioids for long periods of time and not just when they were experiencing acute pain in the short term, average doses rose along with patients' tolerance levels.[9] The mass prescription of opioids led to vast numbers of individuals addicted and in need of ever-higher doses. As opioid prescriptions increased nationally, so did national drug overdose death rates. From 1999–2018, nearly 450,000 people died from an overdose involving an opioid in the United States.[10]

As Mom's tolerance level rose, her recreational prescriptions became pricier. While Mom said the move to Mexico was the product of a divine promise and that she was moving to be with Alex, I also suspect that she found the draw of cheaper and more accessible drugs to be a factor. After all, most of her nights were spent not with Alex but out on the streets getting her supply.

And it was in Tijuana that Mom made the switch to black tar heroin.

When Alex would leave for work at dusk, Mom would take the two of us out on night drives. We would

---

8   Ibid.

9   Gery P. Guy et al., "Vital Signs."

10   "Understanding the Epidemic," Centers for Disease Control and Prevention, updated March 19, 2020.

endlessly circle the same couple of blocks, waiting until we spotted a dealer in the shadow of a building. Fumbling and shaking as she gathered her pesos from the cup holder, she would roll down the window and place her order. In return, she'd receive one or more small, uninflated, and tied balloons. The balloons could easily fit under one's tongue or in the cavity of one's cheek. If you are pulled over by the cops and don't want to get busted, you can swallow the balloons and retrieve them down the road, heroin still intact. I didn't know that what Mom was taking was heroin when I was a kid, though. I only knew that she was taking something cheaper and stronger than what she had taken before. The stack of books I read on the opioid epidemic in college filled in the rest of the details.

As our night drives became more frequent, so did our desperation to make money. Mom had been unable to justify to Alex where the money he had given us had gone. He began to withhold the stipend. They began to yell at each other. Mom began to threaten to leave. I'd sit in the shadows at the top of the stairs and listen to their feuds, worried that Mom would say something to get us kicked out onto the street. I was viscerally aware of the precarious nature of our situation.

With no income, we were forced to drum up money in other ways. Trading in my hopes to re-enroll in school, I became Mom's sales partner. Each day we selected a few of our personal items to sell on street corners or in the daily markets that cropped up throughout the city. Each morning we set out with a bag full of our belongings and a mission to make enough money to buy dinner and Mom's supply later that evening.

Mom would question me each morning in search of expendable belongings. "What do you have that we can sell? Do you have any VHS tapes you can part with? Any stuffed animals?"

Each morning, I'd stand in the middle of my room looking upon my possessions, evaluating them. Initially, the exercise was easy enough. There were some stuffed animals or some action figures that I could part with. "We can sell these!" I'd offer.

The task became more and more difficult each day, however, as I saw my possessions dwindle in number. I imagined what it would be like to have nothing a week from that point in time. I decided to hide some of my belongings under a pile of dirty clothes where Mom wouldn't find them.

Standing on street corners, I made practical use of the Spanish I had picked up from talking with Alex's family and watching local television. Mom's desperation became my own as I sold my favorite belongings to strangers on the street, desperate to make enough money to afford that night's dose. "*Muy barato*, very cheap," I'd announce to all within earshot, gesturing to my toys and spare clothing.

Initially, I had felt ashamed and embarrassed of our situation, just as I had the year prior when Mom and I knocked on church doors in search of food. I should be in school, and Mom should be at work, I chided myself internally. I felt so pitiful standing on a corner, begging strangers to buy our stuff. I imagined how pitiful we looked to passerby and was hesitant to approach anyone, to reveal to them the depths of just how much we needed a sale. I didn't want to display our desperation, didn't want to guilt strangers into buying things.

A few nights without dinner or Mom's supply, though, quickly weakened any misgivings I had. I evolved into a confident saleswoman, skilled at packaging our sob story to maximize sales. I knew my suffering was profitable, and I exploited it to my advantage in any way I could— anything to avoid the scenario of Mom not getting her supply. Without her supply, she would be some mixture of sick, angry, and/or depressed, and I could not bear to see her that way.

We were trapped in a cycle of desperation, and by the time we realized it, there seemed to be no way out. We scraped by day by day. At night, once we made our sales quota, was the only time I could relax and breathe. There was little enjoyment in those days and lots of fear. I feared for Mom's health and my own. I feared for my future. I feared we would have to choose between eating or Mom's supply. My days were dominated by these anxieties that never permitted me to rest.

Whenever I felt self-conscious about my sales tactics, I often encouraged myself by reminding myself that I'd likely never see my customers again. I got so skilled at my position that I became the de facto lead saleswoman. At times, Mom would not even accompany me to the street corner to set up shop. I'd do it all myself while she ran errands or got her supply or sought out money in other ways.

I learned to greet passerby sweetly and express to them the lowness of our prices, assuring them that they wouldn't find better deals elsewhere. Mom learned to use me as an emotional plea for financial support.

"I need enough money to feed my daughter," she pleaded to anyone who made eye contact.

I learned that the best targets were American tourists over the age of twenty-five and middle-aged women; I could nearly always get a sale from them. I found American tourists to be a good target since many, after recognizing a fellow American, were grateful for the sense of familiarity. I say American tourists over the age of twenty-five because American college students were too rowdy and too drunk a bunch to conduct business, and their money was already earmarked for the casinos, bars, and strip clubs. I'd watch nightly as they poured in and out of the Hard Rock Cafe and the casino across the street, their arms thrown around women wearing tall heels as they stumbled through the beer-soaked streets shouting loudly in English. Middle-aged women, on the other hand, nearly always felt sorry that a kid my age was stuck on the streets offloading my toys in the hopes of having a hot meal that night.

I had come to view strangers in this one-dimensional way: did they look like someone whom I could persuade to buy something? Strangers became life rafts, individuals that I needed to emotionally manipulate in order to stay afloat. I learned how to charm them, to compliment their style or their intelligence, in order to get what I needed.

After just a few weeks, we had exhausted our store of toys, clothes, furniture, knickknacks, and home decorations. While I had wanted to hang onto some of my most favorite toys that lay hidden under the clothes in my room, Mom eventually talked me out of them.

"Are you sure you have nothing left?" she asked me. "Nothing at all that we can sell so that I feel okay tonight?"

I sold my Scooby-Doo Mystery Machine and the complete gang of action figures for a minuscule fraction of what they were worth to me. As I watched a father walk away with my Mystery Machine, which he told me was for his son of about my age, I struggled to hold back my tears. I became overwhelmed by the fact that I had little left to my name materially and was unsure if I ever would again.

I was mad that I had to sacrifice all that brought me joy, safety, and comfort for Mom's needs. But I didn't tell her this. I swallowed my anger, dried my tears, and got back to work. Looking back on this, I am not sure why I didn't express my dissatisfaction. Perhaps I understood the depth of Mom's bodily need for her dose that night and knew that complaining would not satiate it. Or perhaps I didn't want to add any unnecessary stress to an already stressful occasion. Either way, I had nothing left to my name save a couple of outfits, a bed to sleep on, and my stuffed bear Girl. I was thankful that her clothing was tattered and torn; she would not be worth anything to anyone else.

Once we had run out of belongings to sell, we knew we had to adjust our business model. Mom and I spent the next year frequenting Tijuana's many pop-up markets to buy merchandise that we could then flip at a profit. Our strategy was to go near the end of the market day when sellers would be more willing to make a quick sale. We'd buy DVDs, CDs, stuffed animals, toys, clothes, watches, and more at cheap prices we'd coerced out of fellow vendors.

Throwing down a well-used blanket a handful of blocks away from the formal pop-up markets, I'd array our merchandise in a familiar pattern: DVDs and CDs lined up neatly at the front, clothes folded and displayed along the sides of the blanket, and the rest of our miscellaneous items arranged in the center. With so much instability in my daily life, I appreciated this systematization of our process. It was one of the few things that I had control over.

We took pride in our business and noted what sorts of items we were able to sell quickly and with a decent profit. We accepted both pesos and American dollars so no customer would be excluded from buying something. The next day, we would apply what we had learned about local demand and seek out more of those types of merchandise. For instance, I once bought several fancy lighters off of a guy at a market at the equivalent of a dollar apiece. They were solid metal, rectangular lighters whose top you would flick open before striking the wheel with your finger. The exteriors of the lighters were decorated with representations of flames, motorcycles, skulls, flowers, scantily clad women, and the Mexican flag. These lighters sold faster than any product I had moved before, and we sold them at five times the price we bought them for. I swear we sold all of them within our first few minutes of opening up shop on a busy corner.

Just by happenstance that very night, I was walking by a local store—the equivalent of the Dollar Tree in the United States—when I glimpsed through the window a whole bin of these lighters in the center of the store. There were hundreds and hundreds of them, and I was electrified. I immediately set off to find Mom. We came back to the store with all of the money we had to our names, save a few dollars in pesos that we stashed for dinner. We bought as many as we could; we filled bags. I felt so blessed that night, so fortunate to have walked by the store.

Mom and I raved about our haul over dinner at a local Chinese buffet. Our plastic bags filled with lighters sat on the tabletop. We admired their different designs and rejoiced in their promise of economic security for the next week, as we stuffed ourselves with chow mein.

The good times were few and far between, however. While we had some lucky nights when we made a profit greater than our dinner and Mom's supply expenses, these moments were rare. Once the store stopped selling the lighters, we were back to buying miscellaneous items at local markets and flipping them on street corners. Money was so tight that we often could only afford to put a gallon or two of gas in our car at a time. We watched our mileage religiously, praying that we could make it through the day without breaking down. There were more than a handful of times when we ran out of gas a couple of blocks away from the station.

Running out of gas became such a fixture of our life in Mexico that we developed a ritual for dealing with this frustrating reoccurrence. First, Mom would curse the aging contraption and our lives' circumstances. I would sigh. Second, I'd jump out of the car, sulk my way to the rear, and begin to push. Mom would hang her head out of the driver's side window, cheering me on as she steered us toward our destination. The sight of an eight-year-old pushing her mom's car down the road would often attract the assistance of one or more passerby who would join me in the rear of the car and help push.

The success of the endeavor of delivering our car devoid of gas to the station pretty much depended on this kindness from strangers. This was the crucial third and last step. I wasn't all that strong.

"*Muchas gracias, señores,*" I'd smile and say to our kind gentlemen helpers.

"We forgot to put in gas," I'd tell them in Spanish, laughing off our situation.

If we didn't have the money we had set aside for food or some other necessity to use for gas when we arrived at the station, we'd set up shop right at the pump. Mom would pop the trunk, I'd retrieve the blanket, and we'd arrange our items of the day in a pleasing array. "*Necesitamos un poco de gasolina*," I'd say, directing strangers filling up their tanks toward our makeshift storefront.

We lived with Alex off and on. He hated Mom's drug use but loved her deeply. They fought, he drank himself to sleep in his boxers, he went to work, and we hit the streets to buy and sell. When they fought, they fought behind closed doors. While I did not know how the fights progressed, I knew they usually ended with Alex giving Mom some money that she promised to use for our necessities.

Alex always wanted to believe the best about Mom, wanted to believe she'd wise up and stop blowing all of our money. But Mom would go out that same night to buy her supply, and I would often come along. By then she knew her dealers by name, greeting them with a smile as they approached our parked car. If we had extra money after she bought, we'd go out for one of my favorite meals: french fries at the casino or a pizza pocket from the 7-Eleven.

I always went with Mom to buy her supply because I didn't like to spend much time alone with Alex. The few times I did stay home with him, he sat and drank beer while complaining about Mom.

"Every time I give her money," he told me one afternoon when it was just the two of us, "she goes out and spends it on that *stuff*." He spit the word "stuff" out with as much disdain as he could manage.

I nodded silently as he continued, "You know, your mother, I love her so much, but sometimes she just drives me mad." I didn't know what to reply, so I stared back at him as he took a swig from his fifth Corona that afternoon.

"At night, when I am not home, where do you both go? Does she see other men? Does all the money go toward that *stuff*?"

"I don't know," I replied unconvincingly. Alex let out a sigh.

I didn't like to be interrogated about where Mom had been and what she had been doing. I refused to betray her confidence. On top of that, having grown up never meeting my biological father, I wasn't used to having a man in my life. It felt strange, and I didn't know how to relate to Alex, and I didn't try to. I rarely talked to him, and I didn't know much about him other than the fact that he desperately wanted to go to the United States and had been a police officer until he had gotten into a horrible motorcycle crash that took him months to recover from. Even though Alex and I weren't very close, I could always tell that he worried about me. I'd often catch him looking at me, his brow creased, his head hung low as Mom and I pulled away. His eyes seemed to apologize that he couldn't do more to secure me a more stable life in Mexico.

On the rare times when their fights ended with Alex refusing to give Mom money, we found ourselves living on the streets for a couple of days. I was never sure if Alex kicked us out or if Mom was using our sudden homelessness as an emotional bargaining tool to make Alex give in. Mom had pulled similar stunts with my brother Jay after he moved out of our apartment in Murrieta Hot Springs, claiming that if he didn't help her with the bills, we were going to be evicted.

There were nights when Mom and I slept in the car or stayed up all night sitting in a restaurant or roaming the streets. On a particularly cold night, we used some extra money we had to rent the cheapest room in a motel in town. I had been so excited to have a bed to sleep in, but as soon as we entered our room, I realized we should have taken our money elsewhere. The room was alive with movement, and once we turned on the single naked bulb that dangled from the middle of the ceiling, cockroaches dove under furniture or scuttled toward the various holes in the wall. The single lightbulb illuminated the room just enough to make out the stains on the mattress and the scrawled writing on the walls. I wrapped my arms around myself as I backed out the door.

"Mom, I don't want to stay here. I'm scared of them," I choked out as I gestured toward a cockroach hanging out in the corner of the room.

"Honey, we spent all our money on this room. And I'm so tired . . . Just try not to think about them, okay?"

"Okay," I muttered, taking hesitant steps back toward the room and holding my breath.

I sat up all night terrified, my ears prickling at any noise that suggested an approaching cockroach or some other unseen horror, flinching at any foreign sensation on my skin. I curled myself into Mom's chest, willing myself to become tiny, wishing that I wouldn't exist or, at minimum, be conscious. Mom was unaware of the depth of my horror. She was in a deep slumber, a consequence of her nightly drug use.

I never saw Mom take the drugs. I only interacted with her afterward. She was very careful about that. Jay tells me that Mom often cautioned him during his teenage years against using substances, detailing their dangers. Perhaps she wanted to insulate me from her reality of routine substance use and protect me from falling into a similar pattern. Or perhaps she was ashamed and did not want to be witnessed.

I was only really scared by Mom's drug use once. It was a late night, and we were driving around town when she began to grow increasingly paranoid.

"Someone is following us," she announced. "We need to hide."

"Following us? Who?" I asked, checking the side and rearview mirrors of the car.

"Not safe here," I heard back. "We need to get off the main road where they can't find us."

I checked all of the mirrors again. No other cars were near us; no one was on the street. I could just make out the sound of barking dogs in the distance.

Mom turned off the main road, meandering into a quiet neighborhood. Parking in the shadows of silent houses, we waited, holding our breaths for the danger to pass. I tried to comfort Mom, but I didn't quite know how. I didn't know how to help her fight an invisible terror.

"I don't see anyone," I offered.

"Oh, they're there," she murmured back, lost in thought.

During a particularly long period of separation from Alex that lasted a couple of months, we spent a series of nights without shelter, immersed in the frigid air of wintertime without proper clothing. Mom and I got pneumonia, or so we assumed. We began to get weak and feverish. A hard, unrelenting cough coupled with chills racked my body continually. Without money to see a doctor and not knowing how to treat our ailments, we were able to secure a discount on a hotel room from an owner who felt bad for us.

At least this room doesn't have cockroaches, I thought to myself as I collapsed onto the bed and completely lost track of time and the outside world. My only sense of the passage of time was the distance between the moments when I had to roll out of bed to cough up multicolored phlegm in the bathroom.

I could just barely make it to the bathroom, I was so weak. As soon as I'd shut the door, I'd let my legs collapse beneath me and crumple onto the cool tiles, lifting my head off the floor to cough when needed. I gazed with both wonder and terror at abstract paintings of red, green, brown, and red phlegm in the toilet bowl, searching for shapes in the water just as I had searched for shapes in the sky with Angelique more than a year ago. I wondered if dying from pneumonia would be more peaceful than drowning. Once my heaving ebbed, I'd flush my artwork down and trade places with Mom.

Mom and I sat in that bare hotel room in silence for the most part. It was only punctuated by our violent coughing and Mom's occasional encouragements that we were going to be okay. She was sicker than I was. I now recognize that that was likely because she was going through withdrawals at the same time. There was little to do to distract me from my despair, as there was no television nor radio.

Days passed and then weeks. Alex came by to give the hotel owner some money for our room after we had managed to get him on the phone and explain what had happened. When we got hungry, whoever was strongest would stumble out of the hotel to the nearest *tienda* or food truck to buy whatever was cheapest with the pesos Alex had left us at the front desk. Most nights I ate fries with ketchup from the food truck out front. Those fries kept me going; they were the one bright spot in my days. I honestly credit them for my eventual healing.

There were a couple of nights when I legitimately thought I might die. My cough and the pain that followed had been getting progressively worse, and without medical attention, I didn't know what I needed to get better. I didn't know if I'd get better at all. No one else knew we were in the hotel room, holed up and seriously sick. Alex was still mad at Mom, and I don't think he understood how sick we were. At times I would frightfully imagine a scenario where we both succumbed to our sickness and died in the hotel room only to be found days later. I was terrified of dying unknown and isolated like this at eight years old.

In her moments of lucidity, when her migraine, shaking, and coughing subsided, Mom would try to comfort me.

"It's going to be all right, just a matter of riding it out," Mom would try to reassure me. "Want to hear a story?"

This would get my attention. "Yeah," I'd choke out through the tears that caught in my throat.

Mom's stories always featured female heroes who, like the Scooby gang, defeated monsters and villains up to no good. While the odds were always stacked against the heroine, she always made it out. Somehow, we made it out too. About a month after we first checked in, we checked out of the hotel room thankful to be alive. I felt overwhelming luck and gratefulness flow over me. Many describe this as feeling blessed, a sense of having taken on daunting odds and come out on top. Just as in the moments after I had drowned, I was in disbelief that I had survived, and I was thrilled. I emerged from the hotel feeling that if I could beat pneumonia, I would find a way to make it on the streets of Tijuana.

We had less than twenty dollars to our names when we checked out of the hotel and went to see Mom's supplier. We were both determined to come up with a way to make money more quickly than trying to turn a profit on stuffed animals and DVDs.

"Mom, why don't we go to the casino? We beat death here at the hotel. Why not see how far our luck goes?" I was feeling unusually sure of myself, confident in my newfound ability to defy the odds.

"What's a kid like you going to do at a casino?" she laughed, her brow furrowed as she tried to figure out what exactly I was suggesting.

"The races! They have horse races, right? Let's go check out the horses and put our money on the one that looks like a winner," I suggested.

Mom placed bets on the horse of my choosing: a brown horse with deep, soulful, chestnut-colored eyes and rippling muscles. I glued my eyes to my horse and watched in awe as we slowly pulled into the lead. Holding my breath, I listened to the announcer excitedly narrate the last lap to the captivated audience. Our horse was neck and neck with another, one was in the lead, then the other. Our horse won by a mere foot. Mom's jaw dropped; I squealed in glee.

We left that night with around one hundred dollars that I won at the races. It was a miracle we didn't lose the only money we had to our names. We both knew it was not a dependable way to earn money, however, so we never went back to the casino again. Mom took me to get a burger from my favorite vendor to celebrate. We sat under the white Arch of Tijuana that welcomed tourists to Tijuana's downtown area, munching on our burgers and enjoying a nearby mariachi band. The next week Mom began to have sex for money.

It was getting colder, and we needed to rent a place to stay. There was a series of streets downtown where women lined up each night, chatting with each other as gawking men passed by. Tall in their heels and unfazed by the cool air in their short skirts and sleeveless tops, they lined the sidewalks waiting for their next client. Mom took me with her. We patrolled up and down the street until she found a spot distanced enough from other women to stand. I watched as she unbuttoned the top buttons of her floral shirt.

I stood behind her, pressed up against the building, grateful for the bit of shadow that surrounded me. I was scared. I knew Mom was about to do something with a strange man that she was less than excited to do. Though I did not fully understand the situation, I was distressed on her behalf.

Within the hour, she had a client. I don't remember what he looked like; I don't think I ever looked at his face. Mom walked the two of us to the nearest hotel where they checked out a room for the next two hours. "Stay here. I'll be back in a while," she said to me.

I sat down in the lobby across from the receptionist. No one spoke a word to me.

An hour passed. I was worried for Mom. I had an overwhelming feeling that this guy she was with was dangerous. I hated him. I was fuming at the idea that he was using my mom, that she didn't want to be in this position but felt trapped. I had never felt that level of hatred before. Unable to sit still any longer or allay my worry, I snuck past the receptionist and up toward their room. I was worried Mom would be mad if I knocked, so I sat quietly against the wall opposite the door. Scrunching my knees up to my chest, I wrapped my arms tightly around them and waited as I rocked back and forth. Emerging from the room a half hour later, Mom started when she saw me. I could see sadness in her eyes. The man exited after her and walked away without a word.

After that night, we didn't go back to stand with all the other women. "He was awful, rude . . . I'm not doing this again," Mom had told me afterward. "There has to be another way. We'll make money another way."

Some nights we would walk by the women on our way to wherever we were staying, and I would feel the deepest pang of sadness. I was sad because I knew that some of the women felt trapped and forced into this profession, just like Mom. I could see that some of the women were unhappy, that some were scared of the men that prowled those streets at night. They were all so beautiful. They deserved the world. They deserved to feel safe. Why were we all doomed to wander these sad and rough Tijuana streets?

Mom decided that the way forward was to meet another guy to take care of her. For her, that meant heading to a new city. She liked the idea of a fresh start. We drove along the coastline, enjoying the beach for the first time since moving to Mexico. We spent a day in Ensenada, walking along the shoreline as waves lapped at our feet. When Mom went off to do something, I found myself sitting in a bar and pool hall, ordering *"una botella de Coca Cola, por favor."*

I watched a group of men playing pool. They were placing bets and money was at stake. I fantasized about getting good enough at pool to provide for Mom and myself. I had never played pool before, though.

Mom came back with a guy. They had apparently hit it off, and we all had dinner together. A week later we found ourselves driving up to his house, a modest place on top of a ridge overlooking the ocean. The two of them went off alone. I walked around the neighborhood, enjoying the salty breeze and the sound of the ocean from below. When I came back, I noticed he had been drinking copious amounts of straight tequila. A shot glass ringed with salt lay empty beside a half-empty bottle. He was passed out, and we went to sleep beside him, all three of us sleeping on his king-size bed.

During his slumber, all the coins that had been in his jeans' pockets had wormed their way out onto the bed. I awoke lying on about twenty dollars' worth of coins. In a state of perpetual scrounging, I impulsively collected the coins and stowed them away in my pockets. When he woke up, he knew that I had taken them and glared at me, asking for them back. We weren't invited back.

In the moment, I was merely sad that I was caught. But looking back at it now, I do feel bad. Desperate to avoid spending another cold night wandering the streets or in a haunting low-budget motel room, I had adopted Mom's strategy of taking advantage of men and their money in order to survive. I thought not in terms of right and wrong, but in terms of having or lacking. I found that it was easy for my sleepless eyes to blur the differences between mine and theirs, just as I imagine grumbling stomachs may find it hard to recall why they are not entitled to the food that stocks the endlessly replenished shelves of grocery stores.

The thing with heroin is you have to maintain your dose to feel well, and if you want to get the same euphoria, that feeling of a world devoid of suffering, you have to up your dose. It's an expensive commitment. Without financial support from Alex or some other guy Mom found, there was no way for us to make enough money flipping merchandise to meet Mom's demand for her supply.

Mom needed a job, something that paid decently and consistently.

I'll never know the story of how Mom got her gig working as a coyote for local drug dealers, tasked with smuggling people across the border. I regret not asking. I imagine it was quite the story.

All I know is she came to pick me up one night—I had been staying with Alex's family for a few days practicing my Spanish and playing soccer with the local neighbor kids—and she was ecstatic.

"Come here," she said, wrapping me in a hug. "Our lives are going to change. I got a job. One that pays well."

Pulling back from the hug, I noticed how happy Mom looked. She seemed to be standing taller, as if a great weight had been lifted off of her shoulders. "Mom, that's great! What job?"

"You'll see. We're going to go meet my boss now, okay?"

We got in the car, and she drove us to a compound on the edge of town. Encircled by concrete walls and barbed wire, the compound was intimidating. The one streetlight in sight flickered off and on in the cool night. Mom parked the car half a block away, and we slowly walked toward a metal gate that served as the compound's entrance. There was a rectangle set high above my line of sight that served as the peephole. We were asked what our business was, Mom knew the right words to get us in, and the gate screeched open.

Dogs barked menacingly, yanking at the ends of their metal chains. Men were scattered throughout the compound, staring, coming in and out of the many low concrete buildings that formed a ring around us. Mom was shaking hands and talking business.

"Jorge sent me . . ." I didn't hear a word she said after that. My eyes had fixated on the guns all around me. I had never seen a gun before that moment, and it seemed like just about everyone had one. My breath caught in my throat. Terrified, I stood frozen in place.

To this day, I return to the compound often and unwillingly in my sleep. It always begins with my eyes on the gun protruding from some unknown man's Levi's. Catching my stare, the man reacts violently, yanking

Mom and me by our arms as we stumble across the dirt and scattered bricks. Other men begin to surround us. We are trapped, and they no longer trust us. We must be disposed of.

Mom and I are herded toward the back wall of the compound. Then a gun is extracted from the waistband of the Levi's, aimed, and fired. Just as I feel Mom's grip tighten excruciatingly around my arm and as the first flash of pain racks my body, I wake up calling out and gasping for air.

In reality, after seeing the guns around me I stood, paralyzed and quietly gasping, next to Mom until I felt her yanking at my arm. It was time to go. One of the mustachioed men had given her a set of keys and a page bearing a set of written directions to our new home. Mom's boss was letting us stay at one of his places to give Mom the stable housing she needed to start her job and get back on her feet.

The directions led us out of the city, away from other buildings and people. We drove for miles down a silent dirt road, and just as we rounded a hill, we saw it.

A white, three-story, concrete mansion stood before us, skirted by cacti and surrounded by a tall metal gate on all sides. Lights were positioned along the ground to light up the exterior of the building. It was stunning. Turning the key in disbelief that it was in fact the right key and this was where we were staying, we entered a foyer lined with paintings of gardens and the desert.

The house was elegantly furnished with claw-footed couches, sparkling chandeliers, and tall candles. I had never seen anything like it. Climbing the stairs, we found the master suite occupied by a king-size bed draped in a deep red duvet. Within ten minutes, we were asleep. It was the most luxurious night of sleep we had had in over a year. There was no worrying about the cold, no walking the streets wishing we had a place to stay, no paranoia about cockroaches or weird stains. It was absolutely blissful.

I must have been asleep for nearly a day because it was dark again by the time I woke up. My second night in the mansion was spent exploring the rooms, wondering what sort of bargain had been struck to secure the lavish lifestyle we were suddenly enjoying. Mom refused to say much about it, and I was not one to press. We stayed for days in the mansion undisturbed. I felt as if I had been plucked out of hell and delivered to a private paradise. The fridge was stocked by some unknown party. I enjoyed eggs and ham each morning. I had rice, beans, and corn tortillas for dinner. I was living a dream that I had not dared to imagine during our time on the streets.

Then the check came in the form of a visit near the end of our week in the mansion. Late at night, tires pulled up outside the mansion; the doorbell rang. I peered down from the top of the stairs to see a stranger at the door dressed in blue jeans and a plaid button-down. His watch gleamed in the light of the doorway. He gave Mom her first assignment.

Mom was to prepare our car for smuggling, and the stranger at the door stayed in the house with us to help her do so. Special compartments had to be hollowed out in the car. Convincing lines and facial expressions had to be rehearsed. We practiced reciting reasons why we were crossing the border so as to not raise suspicion among the border officials. I was to act like an untroubled and energetic kid. My role was to lend Mom an air of normalcy, to defray any suspicion. In hindsight, I believe Mom got the job in part because of me. Having a kid helps you pass under the radar.

Leading up to Mom's first border crossing, she thought it would be better if I didn't know much of what was going on, so I spent a few days with Alex's family cooking, cleaning, and watching telenovelas. Even when Mom was not with Alex, I was always welcomed by Alex's family.

Mom picked me up on the day of the job. "You ready to play your part?"

I nodded. "Ready as I'll ever be." I put on my smile and pulled out the bag of candy I brought along to help me play my part of a kid without a worry in the world.

My mind was buzzing with nerves and stress. I didn't know who or what was in our car. I didn't know the penalty for getting caught. While we needed the money, it all felt too risky. I worried about what would happen to Mom if she was caught by the authorities or disappointed her employers.

We picked up fresh churros from a passing vendor as we sat in the line waiting to cross the border. I thought back to that first churro I had had as Mom and I waited in line to first cross into Tijuana together, nearly eighteen months ago.

The wait only served to intensify my stress. I tried to ensure that it didn't make its way onto my face. When we made it to the front of the line, border officials encircled our car, asking questions of Mom and shining flashlights through the windows, their faces severe and unsmiling.

"How long have you been here in Mexico?"

"What is your purpose for going to the States?"

"Do you have anything in your car that you'd like to declare?" Mom fielded the officials' questions, passing documents back and forth as they were requested.

"Pop the trunk," said one official.

Mom slowly bent down as she reached for the latch to bare our trunk's contents to them, a prayer in her worried eyes, her hand trembling. The next few minutes felt like an eternity as they shifted through the contents of our trunk, knocking on different parts of the car, searching for what may have been concealed.

I had ceased to process our situation. My mind went blank, my half-eaten churro clutched tightly in my stiffened hand. Mom was questioned some more, and then we were told to step out of the car. We were under arrest.

I stared unblinkingly, my heart beating fast in my chest as Mom's arms were pulled behind her back. I heard the tightening of metal handcuffs and Mom's sighs and whispered expletives as I stumbled toward the car that was waiting to forcefully escort us to the border jail. I felt an officer's hand on the small of my back. Another officer guided Mom's head down as she lowered herself, handcuffed, into the car. I slid in beside her, our worried eyes staring back at each other and then ahead at the metal grate that separated us from the border officials seated up front.

I didn't know if they had found the secret hold in our trunk or if our car tags were expired or if Mom had an arrest warrant out for her in the United States or if we did not have the appropriate documents to cross the border. I was too scared to ask Mom for fear of further incriminating us. The only thing I was confident in was that they didn't find a person in our trunk. I'm sure I would have noticed the commotion of that scenario, even paralyzed with stress and fear.

We sat silently in the back of the border patrol car looking at our laps. Arriving at the border jail, we entered a fluorescent-lit, concrete room. The front desk staffer sat protected behind a plastic window reinforced by rusting metal bars. Mom's hands were loosed to fill out paperwork. I noticed with alarm that an officer holding a semiautomatic rifle across his chest stood in the corner opposite us. I stared blankly at the front desk staffer, reminding myself to breathe.

When Mom finished filling out the paperwork, we were escorted down a dark and damp concrete hall. There was no one else in sight. The officer stopped in front of an empty cell, shut off from the world by a thick, metal-barred gate.

"In you go," the officer said in a thick, gruff voice, tobacco wafting off his breath.

The gate clanged shut loudly behind us. The officer left without another word.

The walls of the cell were lined with a concrete slab that extended out from the walls about a foot and a half. Damp and well-stained, it was our only place to sit or rest. There was no other furniture in the room, no bedding, just this cold, unending, concrete slab. I plopped myself down on it next to Mom, who sat completely still and silent, staring at the metal bars.

Looking around, I took in the scattered puddles and the cameras occupying each corner of the room. I felt something drip on my head. I looked up to find an intricate web of cracks in the ceiling, seeping water. I scooted closer to Mom, avoiding the forming puddle I had been sitting in. The smell of sewage permeated our cell. I brought my shirt up to cover my nose and mouth. Unwashed metal toilets with no toilet seats sat out in the open in an attached room. There was no door, no privacy.

For the next few hours, Mom and I paced back and forth in our cage. I tried to remain positive for the both of us. "Maybe we can escape," I offered, my voice echoing back at me in our bare concrete confinement. By the time I had finished the sentence, though, I didn't believe it myself. But that didn't stop me from trying.

Perhaps, I thought, I'm small enough to wedge my body through the metal bars of the gate. While the bottom half of my leg wiggled through with some effort, my thighs resisted flattening themselves any further. The bars were too close together. There was nothing we could use to tinker with the lock. Mom was lying down on the concrete slab, clutching her head. I sat down next to her and unleashed my most powerful glare at the camera across from us, willing our captors to feel guilty and release us.

About six feet away from the bars of our cell was a vending machine, filled to the brim with snacks. I began to fantasize about one of the officers coming to offer us food or water from the machine, but no one came. I was still too scared to ask Mom why we had been arrested. I wondered if it was legal to arrest someone my age. Even if it were illegal, I didn't think the officers would ever get in trouble. Mom and I had been frequently harassed by corrupt policemen in Mexico. We had been pulled over and threatened with arrest for all sorts of things: expired tags, suspicious behavior, speeding; the list goes on. Once they threatened arrest and saw the panic in Mom's eyes, they'd offer her an alternative: a bribe. We had paid the bribe a couple of times, giving the officers all of the money we had. Often it was below what they had asked for, and we would have to convince them that we truly had nothing else to give them.

Mom offered me comforting words every couple of hours, stroking my hair as we lay with our heads touching on the concrete.

"Mom, I'm hungry. And cold . . ." I trailed off, realizing that me listing my discomforts wouldn't do us any good.

"I know, darling, I know." She threaded her fingers through my hair. "It's going to be okay. I think they'll let us go soon or at least give us food," she whispered.

After hours of lying on the concrete slab with the ceiling's drip slowly soaking my clothes through, the cold had penetrated deep into my bones. My limbs felt hard and heavy as I listened to Mom's slow, rhythmic breathing. Somehow, she had managed to fall asleep after nearly twenty-four hours of us being in the cell.

To this day, I cannot stand the feeling of cold surfaces making contact with my skin. It transports me back to that horrid cell.

We were held for about a day and a half. The first time we saw another officer was when one came to let us out of the cell. "You're free to go."

My limbs were stiff as I pushed myself up from the concrete slab. I staggered over to the bars as the officer struggled with the keys.

Mom whispered under her breath, "Thank you, God."

We gulped down the bottles of water we were given in the lobby. I finished mine without stopping to breathe, realizing just how dehydrated I had been as my mind started to whirl back to life.

Mom and I were escorted to our car. We got in silently, threw one last glare at the officers, and drove back toward the mansion. When we could no longer see the border behind us, we grinned at each other, the euphoria of relief washing over us. Neither of us had thought that we were going to make it out of that dank cell anytime soon.

Once liberated, I decided not to ask Mom for an explanation. I had learned to treasure my ignorance. It provided me with a layer of protection against the harsh reality of our circumstances. I didn't want to know if we were detained because they found the secret compartment or because Mom's checks bounced before we moved to Mexico. If I didn't know what really happened, it didn't feel fully real. Unlike the Scooby gang, I was happy with a few unsolved mysteries.

After our time in border jail, I no longer accompanied Mom to work, nor did we stay in the mansion. While Mom worked as a coyote, I stayed with Alex's family, and she and Alex seemed to be getting along all right again. Our nights were either spent with Alex or in furnished short-term rentals that we rented by the week.

When Mom was at work, my new favorite pastime became lying in bed with Abuelita, Alex's mom, and watching the telenovelas that seemed to be on most channels. Lying on the bed, Abuelita would crochet her blankets while I watched the subtitles diligently, trying to hone my spelling. Because Abuelita knew no English, she pushed me to practice my Spanish. When I couldn't come up with the right words to reflect my thoughts, we communicated through our smiles and hand gestures.

One day with Abuelita was spent sorting through a ten-pound bag of pinto beans. We spent hours picking out the pieces of gravel whose shape blended in so well with the rest of the beans, removing any cracked or deformed beans along with them. Side by side, we quietly sorted bean by bean. We would offer a bean up for the other's judgment at times when we couldn't make the decision between "good bean" and "bad bean" ourselves. These quiet moments with Abuelita are some of my favorite memories from my years in Mexico. I felt safe and at peace when I was with her. Her smile, the way it gathered up the crinkles around her eyes, never failed to warm me and take away the chill of the many Tijuana nights I'd weathered.

When Abuelita was resting, I spent time with Alex's older brother Agosto, who had spent some time in the United States and spoke fluent English. This brought me great comfort. It was important to me that someone understood where I had come from and could imagine the difficulty of my transition to living in Mexico. Whenever Agosto returned home from work, I'd follow him around the house, assisting with chores and listening to his travel stories.

Some nights he'd sit at my side at the dining table, watching me practice my drawing—a new hobby I had picked up with my newfound free time. He sat with me for four hours one night as I painstakingly tried to replicate a seated Scooby-Doo snacking on a piece of pepperoni and mushroom pizza. My drawing turned out mediocre, but Agosto thought it was great, and I was thankful for his encouragement. Agosto and Abuelita were my teachers during the time I spent in Mexico out of school. While I wasn't learning mathematics or geography or reading books, I was learning how to lovingly maintain a household, how to embrace trying new things, and how to speak a bit of Spanish.

Most nights—unless she was working—Mom would come to pick me up from Alex's family's house to take me to wherever we were staying. But one night she didn't show up as planned. Instead, my sister-in-law Teressa and her mom, Carol, did.

Sitting watching *SpongeBob* in the living room, I thought they were ghosts when Alex led them through the door to greet me. The last time I had seen my family I was seven years old; now I was nine. My mind raced as I tried to figure out why they were here in Mexico. I ran up to Teressa, gripping her tightly in a hug. In her embrace, I realized how much I had missed her and my brother. I had barely permitted myself to think of them over the last two years. It was easier to ignore my missing them than to wonder when, if ever, I would get to see them again.

"We're taking you back to the States," Teressa whispered in my ear.

"Where's Mom?" I asked, extracting myself from Teressa's embrace to greet Carol with a hug.

"We couldn't find her," I heard back. While my question was dodged in that moment, I later found out that Alex had driven them to Mom's rented room, where they found her catatonically high, unresponsive. Teressa recalls approaching Mom, who was lying prone on a couch in a dark room devoid of windows, no lightbulbs in sockets to lend light. Though Mom's eyes were open, she didn't respond when Teressa informed her that she had come to take me back to the United States. She had stared back blankly, trying to figure out who Teressa was.

"Where's my brother?"

"He had to work today, but he's waiting up for you. We'll go see him now, just a few hours' drive," Teressa reassured me.

I had one last question. "How did you find me?"

"I called them," Alex told me, looking me in the eyes, "I've been worried, y'know, about you and your Mom . . . I called your brother so that maybe someone could come get you and take care of you." While Alex had indeed called them, he had neglected to give Teressa and Carol a long-term number they could reach him at or a specific place to meet. They had wandered around various taxi lots near the border asking for "Alex the taxi driver" for nearly an hour before they found him in the same lot where I had first met Alex.

I started to pack up my belongings, which was a quick task; by then, I owned only a couple of changes of clothes and a green stuffed animal I dubbed Albert who looked, to me, like a mix between a crocodile and a dinosaur. As I stuffed my belongings into a single black trash bag, I realized I was missing Girl, my beloved stuffed bear that I'd had since the day I was born. Mom had her. It was upon this realization that I started to panic. It took a while for Teressa to convince me to leave Tijuana without Girl— she didn't want to risk going back to see Mom and Mom not letting me leave. I felt like I was betraying both Girl and Mom by leaving them behind. In the midst of all of the chaos I'd been through, Girl had been my constant companion and supporter. Eventually, I conceded to leave without her, just as I conceded to leave without Mom.

I hugged Alex and Abuelita good-bye, unsure of what I was feeling. By that point, I was so used to going along with the flow and not asking questions that I didn't really stop to reflect on the import of what was happening. One of my first thoughts was that I'd finally have access to a reliable bed. As we crossed over the border, I glimpsed the border jail where Mom and I had been detained. I felt a chill dance across my skin as I remembered the coldness of our cell and the hardness of the concrete slab we slept on. I quickly turned away and forced my eyes shut. My last thought before I passed out in the back of the car was that I wanted to know when I'd see Mom again.

We drove hours through the night to reach my brother and Teressa's apartment in Yucca Valley, a small town nestled up in the hills of the Mojave Desert. Each time a bump or curve in the road roused me, I forced myself back to sleep, scared to think of the consequences of my leaving Mexico and Mom behind. I was in shock, numb, horrified that I might be losing my mother. My life was uprooted again—not that it was firmly planted to begin with. I didn't know where I was going, but I don't think I even asked.

We drove up along a winding road that delivered us to the high desert town blanketed in darkness. I glimpsed cacti from the light of gas stations along the main stretch. We arrived at the second-floor apartment that was my new home. Jay came out to greet us.

"JJ!" I yelled my favorite nickname of his, running up to greet him. In the excitement of our reunion, I forgot about Mom for a minute. I felt safe in his embrace, a feeling that had been rare over the last two years.

"Wow, you've gotten so big, so tall!" Jay marveled.

Inside the apartment, Teressa had already inflated a twin-size mattress for me in the second bedroom and laid out a couple of clean outfits that were roughly my size. I was excited about the prospect of having my own room, yet sick to my stomach about the fact that I was excited. I was uncomfortable with the sprigs of happiness that were growing out of my rather dark circumstances. I had left Mom behind. After the grand tour of the apartment, I changed into my new pajamas, and by the time my head hit the pillow, I was out.

When I awoke, the cloud of guilt, confusion, and grief had grown thicker in my skull. I wondered what Mom was feeling; I wondered if she was angry or sad or missing me. I hoped she was okay on her own. I tried to imagine living through the sort of things we did in Mexico alone and couldn't. My worry for Mom's well-being and what she thought of me leaving consumed nearly all my waking hours for the next handful of weeks. I felt like a shell of a person and speaking felt like a chore. But I did eat as much as I could get my hands on. After years of scarcity, I was elated to have access to as much as I wanted to eat. I spent a lot of time listening to questions that Jay and Teressa had for me. I answered some and withheld other answers.

"Were you in school in Mexico?"

"No, I wasn't . . . Mom never found me one. But I did some workbooks for my Spanish," I confessed. Teressa and Jay exchanged worried looks.

"So, what did you do every day?"

"Um, you know, sometimes I helped Mom out and explored the city." I pictured myself standing on a corner selling my toys in the cold. I didn't offer any further description of just how I helped Mom out.

"What does Mom do for work?"

"She has a boss and everything. They like her because she is an American." I was wary of breaking Mom's trust, of painting her as a bad parent, so I talked around her job description. Devoted to protecting Mom, I believed that no one could understand our situation or the pull drugs had over her, so I kept a lot to myself.

Many nights, I could not stop the dizzying swell of my emotions, and I would double over in tears, then nausea. Sitting on the bathroom floor, I'd weep and cough and spit and puke into the toilet, desperately wanting to see Mom again. The pain of separation was unbearable. Teressa held my hair back, speaking soothing words. My brother would gently rub my back in clockwise circles. It was hard to stop this cycle once it began, but I felt compelled to for their sake. I didn't want them to think that they had inherited some sort of nervous wreck—I didn't know whether or not I would see Mom again and figured I might be getting adopted. I was afraid that if I turned myself into too big of a problem, they wouldn't want me. Eventually, I'd be able to lift myself off the bathroom tiles and go to bed.

My heart felt like it was fracturing apart, so when I'd go to bed to try to sleep, I developed a method to hold my heart together. I'd lay flat on my back and cross my right arm across my chest to my left shoulder. I'd do the same for my left arm to right shoulder, resting it atop my other arm. I only realized years later that this was the posture of many mummies lying in their coffins. I had invented it, though, as a way to keep myself together. It felt like I was giving myself a hug, like I was becoming compact and stronger. It was my way of preserving myself to enter my new life after Mexico.

A month after I settled into my new life in the States, I was awoken by a gentle whisper. "Susie, Susie, I'm here."

A hand rested on my forehead, a shadow looming over me. I thought I was dreaming. *It can't be.*

Still, the voice continued. I began to rouse my body from its mummified posture, blinking into the darkness, expecting to awake to an empty room. I had dreamt of a similar occurrence many times already and figured it was only becoming more lifelike.

Finally clawing through the veil of sleep, I turned my head to realize it was Mom sitting beside me.

An indescribable joy filled my lungs in the form of a deep breath, expelling all of the hurt and worry that had built up since our separation. "You're back? You're back. You're back!" I tried out different tones, trying to grasp the reality of what I was saying.

I had never been so surprised in my life. "I'm here," Mom whispered back. "I'll be here when you wake up. Go on and go back to bed."

"No, I can't. How will I know you'll be here when I wake up?" I was terrified of losing Mom again, but she assured me she'd be right next to me when I woke up.

As Mom exited the room, I glimpsed Jay and Teressa's worried faces in the hallway. But I felt the opposite of worried. With a feeling that everything would be okay, I sunk peacefully into a deep sleep.

Mom was staying in a local motel. Composed of just a single row of rooms, the burnt-orange exterior of the motel blended perfectly with the desert landscape at dusk. Mom had hitchhiked from the Tijuana border to our desert town with a long-haul trucker and shown up at our apartment's doorstep at 1:00 a.m. Jay and Teressa had not expected her arrival; they had already begun talks with a lawyer about filing for guardianship. My life in Tijuana, they told me, was not the sort of life I needed. Though I had agreed with them, it had not stopped me from missing Mom terribly.

I spent the next several nights in the motel with Mom, hearing about what had been going on in Tijuana since I'd left and sharing what I'd been up to. We spent our days planning for our trip back to Mexico. So caught up in the sense of relief of being reunited with Mom, I didn't question returning to Mexico with her. At nine years old, I believed it was sensible to be with my mom. I felt like it was my duty. I wanted to be there to support her through the rough times I knew we were bound to have.

We went to the nearby Walmart and bought lots of goods that were on super clearance, planning to take them back down to Mexico to resell them for some extra cash to supplement her job as a coyote. We loaded up on notebooks, folders, American snack foods, and other miscellaneous items we thought might turn us a profit.

Our trip back to Mexico was a secret. Mom made me promise not to mention it to Jay or Teressa during the days I stayed with them. Though I felt guilty for misleading them into thinking I would be staying with them after Mom's visit, I was used to keeping Mom's secrets. If Mom asked, I would do it.

When I stayed over at Jay and Teressa's apartment, I practiced gliding around in my new Heelys they had gotten me in the parking lot. At that point, the Heelys were one of the best gifts I had ever been given, tied for first with my Scooby-Doo Mystery Machine that was sold in Tijuana and a red wagon that never made it to Mexico in the first place. As far as I was concerned, Heelys were a superior form of transportation.

I loved wearing my Heelys when I went to the grocery store with Teressa. I'd peer up and down the aisles, make sure the coast was clear, take a few quick steps for a running start, and then lean back on my heels as I sped down the aisle. It was exhilarating. Those moments in grocery store aisles were the most childlike I'd felt in years, and I loved it. If an employee caught me, I'd apologize, turn the corner, and speed off once again.

After several weeks of staying in the burnt-orange motel, Mom decided it was time to go back to Mexico. She was running out of money, and I could tell she had exhausted the supply she had brought along with her. She was shaking more, her mood swings growing more intense. She had only been able to stay as long as she had because she had recently received her annual check from the Chippewa tribe. Being one-eighth Chippewa, she received a check for just over one grand each year from the reservation.

Mom and I went over to Jay and Teressa's apartment to break the news. Teressa was the only one home.

"We're going back to Tijuana," Mom said to Teressa as soon as she opened the door.

"You can't be serious!" yelled Teressa. "There's nothing for her there. She can't go back to Mexico. She's not even in school there!"

"I'm handling it; she'll be fine. She's my daughter."

"You're ruining her life. You must be able to see that," Teressa implored.

"You're lying!" I heard Mom yell as she slammed the door and ran down the stairs of the apartment.

I had heard all of this from the parking lot where I was enjoying my Heelys. I hated conflict. Any yelling instantly threw me into a dissociative fog as my muscles tensed and teeth clenched. Mom was storming in my direction.

"We're leaving!" she boomed.

I started down the road after Mom, her anger fueling her brisk walk. Once again, I was leaving behind those I loved without saying good-bye. I wish I had had a chance to give Jay and Teressa a hug in that moment, to thank them for taking me in.

Talking to Teressa, she recalls telling Mom to leave, angry that she was being so unreasonable. She had no idea that once Mom left, her plan was to grab me from the parking lot and head back for the border. She thought she would have some time before Mom left to reason with her. Realizing my absence, Jay and Teressa drove around Yucca Valley trying to find us. But we were long gone.

Through a combination of hitchhiking, catching a bus, and walking, we meandered all the way back to the border, carrying bags filled with our Walmart loot to sell. Physically, I have little memory of the journey, but what I do remember are the landscapes. Along the way, I treasured each landscape we traversed, snapshotting them in my mind so I would have them to recall later. The landscapes felt like precious friends to me. I visually caressed the images of passing Joshua trees, gentle golden hills, and looming purple mountains. I was clinging desperately to these solid fixtures of the land, yet my duty and care for Mom was ripping me from them.

While I was thankful to be reunited with Mom, I couldn't help but begin to feel wary at the idea of us trying to make it on the streets of Mexico as we neared the border. I was exhausted. After having had distance from our life in Tijuana, I had realized just how much it was taking a toll on me. In my time apart from Tijuana and Mom, I learned that my life was able to be otherwise, that I could spend peaceful days in a clean home without worrying about my survival.

Crossing over into Tijuana, I held my breath, hoping the second time would be different.

Our life in Tijuana resumed much like it had been before. We bought and sold things on the streets, and Mom would go into work for days at a time, leaving me to stay with Alex's family. Mom no longer told me about her job, and I no longer accompanied her to get her supply.

Mom felt more distant in the weeks after our return. I suspected that she resented me for leaving her behind in Tijuana a few months ago. I began to resent her for possibly resenting me. *Why won't she acknowledge these last couple years have been rough?* Ever since my talks with Jay and Teressa, I felt Mom owed me an apology—or at least an acknowledgment—that I was not living the life of a typical American nine-year-old. She framed her coming to get me in the United States as a rescue mission, yet little changed when we arrived back in Tijuana. Just as she had with Child Protective Services, she could put on a show, but lasting change was hard to come by.

When I was not with Mom or Alex's family, I spent my time wandering the streets of our neighborhood. If I had a couple of spare pesos from Mom, I'd go and spend them on candy in a local tienda. My favorites were the sweet peanut-paste cookies with a red rose on the wrapper: the de la Rosa brand of *mazapán de cacahuate*, or peanut marzipan. As soon as I'd start to open one on my walks, they'd start crumbling to dust in my palm. I had to be intentional about how I approached them, or I'd offer my whole dessert to the day's breeze. Once you manage to get a bite, they have a satiny, luxurious texture as they melt on your tongue like velvet. If you haven't had one, you need one. If you're looking for both entertainment and a challenge, eat yours outside on a windy day.

One afternoon, I decided to walk a couple of miles to the local market where vendors had their tents and blankets out with all sorts of interesting things displayed. At that point, I had accrued a couple of dollars' worth of pesos, so I figured I could get something pretty neat. I browsed through endless displays of toys, stuffed animals, clothes, and movies. Just when I was about to spend all my money on a large cheese pizza, I saw the cage of bunnies.

"*¿Cuánto cuesta?*" I asked of the bunnies' vendor, hoping I had enough with me.

"*¿Cuánto tienes?*" I heard back.

The vendor was willing to give me a deal; he must have been moved by the enthusiasm I was exhibiting. I passed him my handful of pesos. I picked out my black-spotted, white bunny to take home with me. My new friend was dropped into a cardboard box and handed to me.

Looking up at me with its big eyes, I lovingly stared at my bunny as I walked us home. I knew absolutely nothing about bunnies and didn't know how to care for them. I was willing to learn, though. I mulled over potential names in my head but couldn't decide on anything. *It'll come with time*, I reasoned. I had to get to know my bunny more. Until I came up with a name, I simply decided to capitalize Bunny in my head.

I arrived back at Alex's family's house to find Abuelita absolutely stunned that I had brought home a live animal. "*¿Qué es esto?*" she managed to ask between her laughs and gestures of surprise. The crinkles around her eyes were especially pronounced as she smiled at me and Bunny.

I told her of my adventure to the market and how I had met a vendor willing to give me a great price on my new companion. Abuelita brought out a laundry basket for Bunny so they could have more room to jump around. We watched Bunny get to know the sights and smells of their new home for over an hour. Bunny's curiosity was mesmerizing. I began to look around the room more too, imagining what it would be like to take it all in for the first time if I were merely the size of a bunny.

Peering through Bunny's eyes, our home grew more wondrous. The tabletop became an insurmountable mountain, the broom a tall tower, and I a giant.

"You can't keep it. We have nowhere for it to live, no food for it." Mom's realism brought my whole fantasy life with Bunny to a grinding halt.

She was right, and I knew it. I was staying in different places all the time and didn't know how to even properly care for my new friend. If no one was going to help me care for Bunny, I knew that I needed to return them.

Furrowing my brow, I held back my tears and lowered Bunny back into the cardboard box.

"I have to take you back," I choked out.

The walk back to the market dragged on, as such things always do when one is so miserable. I wished Bunny would have a kind and loving home. I wished Bunny stability and regular meals. I wished Bunny a happy life. I was so heartbroken over our separation that I could only repeat "I'm sorry" over and over again as I placed Bunny back in the vendor's arms. I tried not to make eye contact with Bunny as I backed away.

I cried all the way home. As I cried, my despair for Bunny morphed into my own despair. I wanted for Bunny all that I felt was lacking in my own life. Like Bunny, I felt absolutely helpless, dependent on others to give me these things but not knowing to whom to turn.

While Alex's family cared for me a few days out of the week, I still skipped meals, sat in the cold for long hours, and moved constantly with Mom. Rarely with a clean outfit to change into, we moved in and out of Alex's house, to motels, and to apartments in an endless cycle of cold and lice. The worst part was this: Mom never indicated that any of it was going to change.

"When do I get to go back to school? Will I be held back? When will I get to hang out with kids my age?" Mom did not have an answer for me.

"I'm trying, honey . . ." Mom would say after a deep sigh. I hated stressing her out. Once the sighing started, I would choke back my deluge of questions, tears brimming in my eyes.

Jay and Teressa arrived at Alex's family's house late one evening, six months after I last saw them. This time, I knew why they were here. It was time for me to leave Mexico, and Alex had called them—once again—to come get me.

Mom had been increasingly absent, working as a coyote, but it had been longer than usual since I had last seen her. I did not want to leave without saying good-bye again.

"Where's Mom?" I asked to the silent room. All eyes were on me, then moved from person to person as they debated who should tell me.

Alex cleared his throat. "Your mom was arrested earlier this week. Her job, it is dangerous, you know?"

I knew. I imagined Mom back in a cold, damp cell, lying on a concrete slab as her bones slowly turned to ice. I imagined what it would be like to go through that without any company. I imagined it was awful.

"Well, when will she get out? What did they arrest her for?" No one could give me the answers I wanted.

"This means I'm leaving, huh?" A chorus of nods confirmed my suspicions. I had been mentally preparing for this moment, as I doubted Jay and Teressa would let me stay in Tijuana after all they had learned about my life with Mom there.

Alex explained that since Mom was in jail—this time for longer than a couple of days—the foster care system had wanted to step in. Alex used his clout as a former police officer to compel officials to wait a bit longer before putting me in the system. My stomach knotted, and the breath was knocked out of me at the mention of how close I had been to entering the foster care system.

"She has family in the States, let me find them," he had pleaded.

With extra time granted, Alex phoned Jay and Teressa to come get me as soon as they could.

Just as last time, I didn't have much to bring with me: only the clothes on my back and Albert, my green, species-ambiguous stuffed animal. Anything Jay and Teressa had gotten me—the new clothes, my treasured Heelys—had been sold within a week of our return to Tijuana.

"Where's Girl?" Teressa asked, once I had finished throwing my belongings into a black trash bag.

"Oh, Mom had her for a bit, but then she got left at Mom's boss' mansion . . ." I explained, avoiding eye contact. "It's not somewhere we can really go on our own." I pictured Girl seated among men in Levi's with guns in their waistbands. I wondered what would happen to her. I hoped she would live in that lavish mansion for years to come, but reasoned that this was unlikely and she was probably thrown in the trash. She was, after all, not in the best shape of her life. Mom had sewn her back together a half dozen times. Her left eye was hanging on by a single thread, and her once-pink outfit was stained and tattered.

I thought about this as I walked around the house saying good-bye to all of Alex's family, thanking them for all of their help over the years. *I am leaving Mom, again.* This time I knew I could live with the guilt. I needed to put myself back together, just as Mom had put Girl back together many times before.

I hugged Abuelita tight. *"Muchas gracias por todo,"* I whispered in her ear. I wanted to say so much more but didn't know how to express how much the years of her care and love meant to me.

Finally, I thanked Alex. I inhaled the woodsy scent of his cologne one last time, then pulled away to look into his eyes. I didn't know what to say, so we stared silently. Though we weren't super close, I was thankful for Alex's concern. If he hadn't had called my brother, I don't know what would have happened to me. I thought about how if all went well, this would be the last time I would ever see Alex or Abuelita or Agosto.

As we drove through the mariachi-music-laden Tijuana streets toward the border, I was overcome with a sense of finality. I worried for Mom wherever she was locked up, but I couldn't help her. If it weren't for Jay and Teressa coming to get me, who knows what would have happened to me in the foster care system in Mexico.

I was smiling as we crossed the border. I rolled down the window to relish the sweet California breeze.

Since my last time staying with Jay and Teressa, they had moved into a one-bedroom home on two acres of tumbleweed Mojave Desert land, a twenty-minute drive from the town they'd lived in previously. We transformed the long but narrow eggshell-yellow laundry room into a bedroom for me. Jay caught a stray cat hanging around his coworker's house and gifted her to me just before my tenth birthday. Squeak, a calico cat with a heart-shaped spot on her hip, was a great source of comfort to me. Always on my lap, she kept me company as I tried to adapt to my new life.

Teressa passed on to me her love for movies. Our bonding began with us sitting and snacking on the couch together as we watched every movie we could get our hands on. For the year we spent living in the desert, we had well over a hundred DVDs that we'd paw through each weekend to select our upcoming adventure.

Movies provided the perfect escape I needed after my separation from Mom. I loved the feeling of being immersed in an alternate reality where all of my trials and tribulations had never occurred. I loved seeing new places and witnessing the different ways people thought about and interacted with the world and with each other. But even more so, I loved the time I got to spend with Teressa. Sitting on a couch and watching something on the TV felt refreshingly normal and safe.

Mom called on my tenth birthday. She was out of jail, and she was mad that I had abandoned her.

"How could you do that to me? How could you be so selfish?"

I was apologizing through my teary coughing and sniffles when she hung up. The call had lasted less than a minute.

Teressa was immediately at my side, embracing me in a hug.

"What did your mom say to you? What's wrong?" Teressa asked me, her voice thick with worry.

"She's . . . um . . . mad at me. She hung up." I stared at the floor, tears dragging lines down my face. Mom didn't have a stable phone number, so I couldn't call her back, and she didn't call me.

"Want to watch something with me on the TV? Your pick." Teressa's voice brought me out of my head. "We can even have some snacks." I was hooked, thankful as always for the distraction and the company.

Jay and Teressa began guardianship talks immediately afterward, securing the right to call the police if Mom tried to take me back. I was relieved to have this security. There was no way I was going to let myself be dragged back onto the Tijuana streets.

Still, I felt terrible about leaving Mom. I no longer knew who needed to forgive whom. I had thought it was I who needed to forgive Mom, but I began to feel it was I in need of forgiving. Or maybe, I thought, we are both just trying to survive in our own way. My act of survival would be finding stability back in the United States and in school. Mom's was simply to stay alive and to not feel sick, and the drugs helped her do that. They helped her to feel not so sick inside.

I had missed nearly three years of school while I was in Mexico.

After I had been in the United States for a couple of weeks, Jay drove me to our local school where I sat for a placement test as he explained to the administrators the reasons behind the gap in my schooling. While the placement test revealed I was a bit behind on the concepts I needed to know to start the fifth grade come fall, we assured them that I would catch up.

We drove to the nearest Barnes & Noble, where Jay bought me an armful of English and math workbooks covering the material in the third and fourth grades that I had tested poorly in. He also bought me a deck of multiplication flashcards.

"If you learn all these in a couple of weeks," he told me, pointing to the stack of flashcards, "I'll give you a hundred dollars."

"A hundred dollars! All for me?" My mouth hung open in surprise. "Give me a week."

I learned all of my multiplication tables that week. I practiced them so much that they started appearing in my dreams. When I wasn't practicing, I was fantasizing about what I would spend my riches on. As promised, Jay gave me a crisp one-hundred-dollar bill, then drove me to Walmart so I could assemble a new stockpile of toys that would not be sold.

Once I had my multiplication tables down, I turned my attention to the stack of workbooks. When Jay and Teressa left for work, I would sit on the couch next to Squeak and study grammar, punctuation, division, and fractions. I finished the stack of workbooks in just over a month having enjoyed every second of it. I had spent years longing for the opportunity I now had: to be in school, learning alongside other kids my age. At summer's end, I walked into my fifth-grade classroom and picked a seat at the front, ready to learn.

I loved my new life. I relished the fact that I only had to worry about school, as opposed to where I was going to sleep that night or where my next meal was coming from. My new job was to do my homework. No longer was I expected to drum up cash for Mom's supply.

Each morning, I walked a little over a mile along our desert road to reach the bus stop. I was captivated and at times scared of the desert's power. The wind was a constant presence. When walking, I could feel the sharp stabs of sand making contact with my flesh. At home, the wind rattled our windows so intensely I sometimes felt as if we were going to be swept up into the sky like in *The Wizard of Oz*. The wind howled alongside the coyotes at night, and poisonous rattlesnakes occasionally curled themselves up on our doorstep.

On my walks to and from school, I investigated all the different sorts of plants I encountered and chased after tumbleweeds. I investigated the long-abandoned dwellings that seemed to be in abundance. I wondered where the tenants had gone and why they had abandoned their sofa and knickknacks to the ravenous sands of the desert. I wondered where the doors and windows of the dwellings went. Were they taken? Or were they claimed long ago by the desert as the biting sand slowly disintegrated them?

Jay and Teressa each worked long hours on top of their commutes, so I had a lot of time to myself that even homework and desert adventures could not fill. Remembering how good of a speller Mom was, I began to practice new words I encountered, and soon discovered I had a similar knack for stringing letters together. I'd spell new words under my breath as I walked to and from the bus stop, spelling to the rhythm of my steps. As I spelled, I hoped I would one day be as good as Mom was; Jay bragged she could type ninety words per minute with perfect spelling. In the second half of fifth grade, I won my school's spelling bee and advanced to the district-level spelling bee.

For the district spelling bee, I was given a ten-page, single-spaced list of potential words the spelling bee host would be drawing from the day of the competition. Jay stayed up with me most nights to help me practice. If I got one wrong, he'd mark it with a blue check mark, and we'd circle back to it until I got it right three times in a row. I was determined to give my best effort at the competition.

The day of the competition, the contest came down to me and a red-haired boy in a red-and-white-striped shirt and white tennis shoes. We battled back and forth, spelling each word offered to us into the microphone with confidence. The school auditorium we were in hosted over a hundred people, some of them local news reporters. Audience members leaned forward in their chairs as my opponent and I volleyed control of the mic back and forth. I wondered what would happen if we went through all of the words that had been on the ten-page list.

Then my opponent tripped up on the word "anniversary." My breath hitched as I realized I had a chance to claim the win. I spelled out "anniversary" correctly, followed by "centennial," and was announced the district spelling bee winner. My mouth hung open in surprise as cameras flashed. I shook my opponent's hand, and we posed, smiling, for a local news reporter. I was wearing my favorite Scooby-Doo T-shirt, jeans, and Converse for my debut.

I made eye contact with Jay and Teressa in the audience, and we smiled. A fake gold medal was hung around my neck, and I was presented with a trophy and a $500 savings bond.

"What do you hope to do when you grow up?" a reporter asked me. I had never been asked this in a serious way by a stranger before. I panicked.

"Umm . . . I would like to be a surveyor like my brother." I felt like this was a serious-enough answer for a serious question. Truth is, I had no idea what I wanted to do and still don't.

"What's a savings bond?" I asked Jay as we made our way to the car. I was disappointed to learn that the bond was not the equivalent of a check.

When I returned to school after the spelling bee, I was welcomed as a champion. My homeroom teacher threw a little party in my honor, and we all had cake. While my $500 savings bond was ultimately lost in our next move, the experience was invaluable. I had gained confidence. Though I had started the fifth grade at a disadvantage, the spelling bee convinced me that missing a few years of school didn't mean a thing when it came to what I might be able to do in my future.

In my new life with Jay and Teressa, education was my safe haven and school my comfort. With the spelling bee under my belt, I began to view my place in the world differently. No longer was I bound by dismal circumstances. For the first time, I began to see all of the possibilities that lay before me. I knew my life was able to be otherwise.

The summer before I was set to begin seventh grade, we packed up our life in the Mojave Desert and headed north to the forested college town of Chico, California. Jay had started working as soon as he graduated high school and had decided more than a decade later that it was time for him to get his bachelor's degree. Chico was a pretty place with good schools. A town of trees and bikes, littered with coffee shops and pleasant walking paths, Chico was a place where I could breathe deeply without inhaling a mouthful of sand. Instead of exploring abandoned homes, I took in art at local galleries, learned how to bowl, and in the local creek, Teressa taught me to swim. No longer was I in a place where I could walk for miles with no one in sight, nor was I lost in a cityscape vaster than I could commit to memory. With approximately 87,000 people who called it home, Chico was the perfect size.

Our move to Chico, however, was not without its difficulties. Leaving the Mojave Desert meant moving further from Mom to a place she didn't know to look for me. While I had no interest in moving back to Tijuana, I was scared about the idea of leaving the place that promised our only hope of seeing each other again. The only chance for connection we had left was if she called Jay's cell phone number, which he promised me he would never change.

While grappling with this break, I decided to change my name. I had gone by "Susie" for the first twelve years of my life, an abbreviated version of my full legal name, "Susannah." I never liked Susannah. I always felt like it was too formal and too lengthy, plus I didn't like the song lyrics that it often invoked when I introduced myself to others. So when it came time to change my name, I selected the next obvious shortening of Susannah: "Anna." I've gone by that ever since. Given my increased distance from Mom, I figured it was as good a time as any to reinvent myself.

Though I had tried to mentally prepare myself for the move, I still found myself overwhelmed when it happened. The wound of my separation from Mom felt fresh once again. Though I tried my best to put on an air of normalcy—I did my homework, did my chores, and told no one about my strange life in Mexico—I did not feel normal. For the first time, I found myself struggling with depression and suicidal thoughts, just as Mom had throughout her life, and this terrified me. I worried that I was on the same path as Mom. I worried that my brain would become such a dark place filled with suffering that the only way to feel a little at peace would be to dull its functioning, to stop thinking, to place myself in a state where there was no "me."

I still loved going to school and learning, but I couldn't help but think about throwing myself in front of a bus each time I walked home alone. I worried about communicating these feelings and recurring thoughts to Jay or Teressa, so I kept them to myself. I thought that confessing how I was feeling out loud would only make the problem more real, and I wanted to ignore it. Plus, I didn't want to worry Jay and Teressa. The fifteen-minute walks to and from school were incredibly difficult for me, though, as were the nights and early mornings when I found myself unable to sleep. My sleeplessness became so routine that I often found myself awake at 5:00 a.m. watching the early morning local news. For months on end, I watched two hours of local news before getting ready for school each morning. I swear I was probably the most informed twelve-year-old in the city on local happenings.

Halfway through the school year, I noticed that if I timed my walk correctly, I'd intersect with another girl walking to school. The first handful of times we intersected, we walked near each other in silence. As a shy kid in a new town, there was no way I was going to make the first move, but I appreciated her company. Then one day, she broke the silence.

"Hi, I'm Haylee!"

"Hi, I'm Anna," I said, still getting a hang of my new name.

I learned Haylee lived in the apartments at the halfway point of my walk to school. We began to intentionally sync up our walks to and from school. The more we chatted, the more relieved I began to feel. I was thankful to have a friend who looked forward to seeing me each day. It made it easier for me to look forward to each day, too.

Haylee would often walk me all the way home, even though she'd have to double back to go home herself. If we were lucky, by the time we arrived at my apartments, there'd still be fresh cookies in the apartment complex's office. We'd sneak in a couple of times a week, check that the coast was clear, and then load up on chocolate chip and snickerdoodle cookies, despite the "Take One Cookie" sign that was taped to the wall above the tray.

Haylee and I became inseparable. In the afternoons after school let out, we would practice jumping off swings and landing in stylized poses together. We got matching Vans and matching blisters that we earned during our endless strolls through the mall. With no money to our names, we would try on dresses we couldn't afford and accept any and all free samples that Bath & Body Works had to offer.

Around this same time, I met Justin and Lisa. Justin was a youth pastor at the church that sat on the other side of my apartment complex's fence, and Lisa was his wife. Perhaps detecting my loneliness, my science teacher recommended that I attend the weekly lunch club that Justin and Lisa hosted at my school as a way to find community, so I did. I brought my greasy lunch pizza the following Thursday and plopped myself down at a table filled with strangers, muttering a "hello" to those around me. Just as I brought my pepperoni pizza slice to my mouth, Justin screamed. The pizza slipped from my fingers back onto my brown paper tray.

"Hello!" he boomed. "Welcome! Glad to have you here," he said, in between gulps of Mountain Dew. I had never received such an enthusiastic or caffeinated welcome.

Over the course of the lunch hour, Justin ran back and forth across the room, played with the anatomical skeleton in the corner, and made us all laugh with his random observations and general silliness. I hadn't laughed that hard in years—not since I had parted ways with Mom.

Lisa was warm and equally as welcoming. Sitting in the free chair next to me, she spoke to me like an old friend, her voice saturated with kindness, her eyes locked on mine.

"Do we shop at the same store?" she joked, gesturing at my plaid shirt that matched hers.

I laughed, appreciating the icebreaker. "Maybe we can go shop together next time," I joked back.

I was disappointed when the end-of-lunch bell rang. Justin and Lisa were literally the nicest people I had met in my life, and I didn't want to leave their presence. They had—and still possess— this ineffable power to make anyone feel accepted and loved.

The following week, I attended youth group at Justin and Lisa's church. I was anxious to learn more about the God who told Mom to move to Mexico. It had not turned out to be a very wise plan, but I give second chances. I had also always been curious about what would happen after I died, as well as what being "good" entailed. Attending youth group was the first time I got to think about these questions with others.

As with anything in my life that I'm interested in, I dedicated myself wholeheartedly to exploring my new fascination. I read through the entire Bible twice my first year attending. I began to learn guitar so I could be a part of facilitating the musical segment of what felt like a very special gathering. Justin gifted me a beautiful light-wood guitar that I lugged back and forth from home to school to church. In these moments, I often thought about how my brother had found a similar community in church during his teenage years, and how if we were the same age, we might have played in the same band together.

On Wednesday afternoons, Justin and I would sit on the well-worn couches in the hours before service practicing my chords and strumming patterns. When my aching fingers could press down the metal strings no longer, we would eat pizza together in the lobby or slurp down a Mountain Dew. Lisa and I would sit and craft together for hours, talking endlessly. We made duct tape wallets and homemade coasters. When I told Justin and Lisa about what had happened with Mom, they filled my weeks with so many events that I always had something to look forward to. They gave me the gift of making sure I no longer had time to live in the past.

By the end of our first year knowing each other, I considered Justin and Lisa family. I looked up to them. I admired the way they cared for people and appreciated how much they cared for me. Alongside Haylee, they brought joy and a sense of community that I hadn't even realized I was desperately missing into my life.

Jay never stopped pushing me to do my best in school, not even when I was already caught up and at the top of my grade. My first year in Chico, he paid me to work through a pre-algebra textbook and then to read a lengthy biography of Warren Buffett. I liked the math and disliked the biography. Clocking in at over nine hundred pages, Buffett's book hurt my wrists and put me to sleep. Like clockwork, I could be found every afternoon for weeks on end asleep with Buffett's book draped over me like a blanket.

Jay and I now both recognize that I was too young to start thinking about investing, and in hindsight, he should have assigned me a different book. But when I brought home a math problem I didn't know how to do, he'd stay up until he figured it out, determinedly scribbling in a notepad. Sometimes he'd even mark papers I was writing for school, correcting grammar issues. I sometimes disliked his involvement when I was a kid.

"Can we just give up on this one?" I said, gesturing to the final math problem on my homework and the array of crumpled-up pieces of paper on the dining table from our failed attempts to figure it out.

"Nope. We're going to figure it out!" Jay replied without hesitancy.

"But I'm tired, and it's not even worth that many points," I retorted. "My teacher will give me the answer tomorrow."

"But we can figure out the answer tonight," Jay said, refusing to give in. I sighed and slumped into the chair next to him.

I now look back on these moments with deep gratitude. It is a rare thing to find someone who is so committed to helping you thrive. If it weren't for my

brother showing me that I could catch up in school—
and even excel—with a bit of hard work, I would have
never had most of the opportunities I've had this far
in life.

With Jay's support, I attended a charter high school
in five rows of portable classrooms that sat behind
Chico's traditional brick high school. "You'll get a better
education with smaller class sizes," Jay told me.

While Inspire School of Arts & Sciences didn't have
the same architectural grandeur as the high school it
sat behind, it more than made up for it in character.
Inspire was a place that asked us what our dream was
and then told us to pursue it. There was no correct
dream, only a community of people ready to support
whatever that dream may have been. My classmates
were a dedicated bunch—all with at least one passion
they were pursuing. My friend Liv was an engineer, Jude
an artist of many mediums, Allegra a natural and social
scientist, Mikala a ballet dancer and political scientist,
and Angela a mathematician with the gift of making
anyone feel special.

With good luck, Haylee also ended up at Inspire,
and for our first year or so, we commuted together
and lived in the same apartment complex. We traded
in our matching Vans for skateboards. Allegra came to
Inspire a year later. Though we had known each other
previously, it wasn't until her arrival at Inspire that
we became close. Curly hair cropped close to her face,
Allegra could always be found in jeans, Converse, and
a rad T-shirt picked up from a thrift store.

During my four years at Inspire, I marveled as student artwork spread along the sides of our classrooms and decorated our doors, a stark contrast to the brick and tan walls of my previous school. Each painting spoke to some aspect of our shared experience. The doors told stories about what sort of knowledge might be gained inside. A small garden was planted then populated by sunflowers taller than me. Inspire was not a place that held us students captive, but a home for us to build as we learned together and from each other. Allegra's and my contributions to our shared home were a microwave and toaster oven that our English teacher let us stack on top of one another at the back of her classroom. Without a cafeteria of our own, the double-decker microwave and toaster oven became a beloved student hangout, a culinary oasis. Nothing says home like freshly toasted quesadillas or reheated chili.

Allegra and I had nearly all of our classes together, and when we became eligible to take courses at our local university, Chico State, on top of our high school courses, I convinced her to take Mandarin with me. A couple of times each week, we briskly walked the half mile to Mandarin class after high school let out. For two people who barely studied, we did pretty well. Allegra and I spent two semesters learning with Lǎoshī, our teacher, and a handful of twenty-somethings in old, luminescent classrooms.

Constantly trading snacks back and forth along with whispered conversations, I imagine we were quite the nightmare to deal with. Lǎoshī was a very patient woman. She even put up with us through our scooter phase when we each rode Razors with light-up wheels to class.

"Ha-ha! What is that?" Lǎoshī exclaimed when we first rolled our matching scooters into the classroom.

I paused, assessing whether I had the vocabulary at my disposal to even attempt to explain in Mandarin. I did not. "These are our scooters. They light up. Allegra and I got them last week during Black Friday," I explained. "You do any shopping?"

"No, I don't do that," she said, still beaming in our direction. Though we were somewhat of a handful at times, Lǎoshī always seemed happy to see us and entertain our youthfulness.

In addition to Mandarin, I was also taking courses on religion and politics at Chico State, many of them recommended to me by Jay, who was working on his degrees in religious studies and natural sciences. Never before had I felt so excited to learn. I was just beginning to realize the amount of stuff out there that I could know, and it was invigorating. In my final year of high school, Allegra, Jay, and I managed to get a spot in one of the most interesting courses I've ever taken: a course on secret societies.

We read books on the structure of secret societies and their gatherings. As our final project, our class created our own secret society. A group of ten or so of us wrote a small book on the rituals, practices, ideas, and members of our society: The Society of the Unified Beings, a colorful UFO cult that Jay and I dreamed up after attending a UFO conference earlier that year in our old home, the Mojave Desert. For the course final, we were tasked with kidnapping our professor from his home and initiating him into our society.

We led our blindfolded professor to the base of a lit cross up on a hill in the middle of dry grassland. It was nearly dark—we had barely enough light left to read our notes under the dark-blue sky. The muted light of the blue hour and the surrounding quietude of our landscape gave the scene an especially eerie feeling. I listened to my classmates' ragged breathing as we joined together in a circle at the top of the hill.

"Do you, Professor, promise to uphold the rites and responsibilities of The Society of the Unified Beings?" boomed the voice of my classmate.

"I solemnly promise."

"Good. We will now remove your blindfold." Our professor peered through the dark, trying to put together where he was.

"Are we in Bidwell Park?"

"No questions, please. Do you, Professor, promise to commit to heart the wisdom contained in the Book of Changes?"

"I do!"

"Then, please, place your hand on the sacred text and repeat after me: 'I will pave the way, through the masterful use of my talent and life . . .'"

Our professor echoed the commitment as I dusted him with our "sacred" powder. Another classmate sprinkled him with water.

"'. . . for the arc transcendental change in natural consciousness required to prepare all beings for the inevitable collective reunion. All work of our order and all my labor is done for the complete pleasure of the

Unified Beings,'" our professor completed his pledge, grinning ear to ear.

"We welcome you," my classmates and I intoned in unison. After a communal recitation of various homemade poems in honor of the Unified Beings, we left our mountaintop in favor of greasy pizza and beer—for those of us who were of age—downtown.

When my family moved to the small mountain town of Magalia my second year of high school, my commute to school grew from a half hour to an hour and a half each way. I would catch a bus just before 6:00 a.m. while it was still dark out. Many early mornings, I'd glimpse a skunk's reflective eyes or hear a rustle of life in the plant growth that surrounded me. I'd stand in the otherwise silent night, illuminating my immediate surroundings with my phone light, until I'd see two tall headlights round the corner and hear the telltale huffing of the bus's brakes as it came to a halt in front of me.

While Magalia offered us a peaceful forest environment and housing prices we could afford, the commute was exhausting. On lucky days, I would catch a ride home with Jay after he got out of his college courses or Teressa after she got off work. On not-so-lucky days, I would have to take the regional bus home that dropped me a mile or so downhill from my home during that time of day. The lengthy commute was worth the education I was getting, though, as well as the friends I made along the way. I treasured being able to go to a school I loved, and it was on my early morning commute that I met Mikala.

Mikala lived in lower Magalia and would get on the bus just a couple of stops after me in the morning. Most of the bus riders at this early hour were middle-aged construction workers, so Mikala and I were a clear match for conversation and company. After a few bus rides together, I found myself looking forward to the next early bus ride with Mikala. When our bus finally arrived in Chico, time permitting, Mikala and I developed a ritual of going to Starbucks to caffeinate before walking the last half mile to Inspire.

On the nights I had class at Chico State, however, there was no longer a bus I could take home at such a late hour. I began spending the night at Justin and Lisa's house a few nights a week. Their home became my second home. When I first began staying over, I moved into a makeshift bedroom Lisa constructed sandwiched behind the living room couch and the wall. Christmas lights encircled the perimeter of my bedroom, which consisted of a made-up mattress on the floor and some floor space for me to set my books and other belongings.

"I'm sorry, it's not much, but we wanted to make you a space."

It was perfect. I could feel all of the love that was put into it as I lay beneath the multicolored Christmas lights warmed by my new blankets. A couple of months later, my room migrated to the dining room area. A makeshift Styrofoam wall was put up and garnished with my favorite Christmas lights. In the mornings when I emerged from my room into the kitchen, I'd often find Justin cooking me one of my favorite breakfasts: eggs, soy chorizo, cheese, and hash browns in a flour tortilla with ketchup. With a to-go cup of coffee in my hands and my breakfast burrito, Justin would drop me off at school as content as I could be.

Mom had rarely ever cooked for me. I only remember her making me an egg sandwich a handful of times; Jay, Teressa, and I rarely ate breakfast together. So I found it incredibly novel to be cared for in such a way in the mornings. It was an amazing feeling. It was the sort of feeling I imagined kids felt when a parent packs their lunchbox full of their favorite foods.

I didn't formally decide I was going to apply to college until the summer before my last year of high school. While I of course loved learning, I had never thought seriously about college. In my mind, college was not only something that was financially unattainable, but also a daunting and complex process. It wasn't until that summer that Jay and I got serious about learning for ourselves the process for applying to private colleges. With no one in our lives who had gone to college before Jay enrolled at Chico State, we started from scratch. The plan: I either needed to get a full ride to a private university, or I was going to attend a state school in California where I could get need-based financial aid.

Though I had been living with Jay and Teressa for over seven years, they had never formally become my guardians. Because of this, I was considered financially independent when applying to colleges. I did not have a dime to my name, and Jay and Teressa did not have any money saved up for my college education. Even if we did have some money saved up, it would have been nothing compared to the ticket prices of the colleges I was looking at. They all seemed to be upwards of $70,000 per year. I imagined students eating freshly made pasta with grated gold flakes.

Jay and I began looking at schools that offered financial aid based on the applicant's financial status. We also strategically looked at schools that had a variety of acceptance rates, so that I could take a chance applying to some while still having some sure acceptances. We inputted everything into a sprawling spreadsheet that we titled "The Mega College Spreadsheet." I would often find Jay in his armchair awake late into the night inputting acceptance rates, average test scores, average GPAs, deadlines, and financial aid stats into the spreadsheet. Other nights, I'd find him asleep in his chair, laptop balanced precariously on his knees, spreadsheet open.

Once I finalized the list of ten or so colleges that I was going to apply to, I spent the next several months painstakingly writing draft after draft of application essays. Jay spent most of his nights reading over what I had written, helping me talk through my ideas and come up with the best draft possible.

"Don't be afraid to be vulnerable in your personal statement," he'd remind me.

"I don't want to come off as a sob story or a charity case, though . . ." I'd say, voicing my anxiety.

"You're not. You are who you are, and you've had certain unique life experiences. Use them."

"Okay, I'll give it a try." I told the colleges I applied to about Mom and our life on the streets of Tijuana, concluding:

"Although my life's early hardships once seemed like the knell of a bell signaling the end of future hoped for, it is those experiences that I have to thank for getting me to where I am today. They are the basis of my identity, the reason for my compassion, and the foundation of my worldview."

I told them how I loved to learn more than anything, how knowledge made me feel safe, happy—even excited. Most importantly, I told them that education's highest virtue is its ability to foster improvement in the world at large. I sent my application early to Georgetown University's School of Foreign Service and applied to all my other colleges at the normal time.

After having spent many dozens of hours figuring out the college application process and applying, I had allowed myself to hope that I would get into an excellent school with a full ride, but I knew the statistics and how unlikely it was. I tried to push any hope from my mind, but it was sticky. I tried to not tell too many people where I had applied since I didn't want the pressure of telling them I didn't get in.

In mid-December, a letter from Georgetown arrived. My hands were trembling when I picked it up from our dining room table. I took the letter to my room and closed the door. I struggled to open the envelope, nearly tearing it in half. First, I saw a fancy crest and then the word "Congratulations!" I gulped down air as my jaw hung open. I stood for several minutes in the middle of my room, stunned. I knew that my life had just changed, but I didn't quite understand how. I stumbled into the kitchen to share the news with Jay and Teressa.

"Wow!" they declared in unison.

"Yeah, wow," I repeated back.

"Congratulations!" said Teressa, bringing me into a hug.

I read the letter over and over again in my bed later that night, unable to sleep as Squeak lay curled up beside me. I felt a pang of sadness as I realized that going to college meant leaving her behind. I had rarely spent more than a few days without seeing Squeak since I was ten years old. I hoped she would forgive me. I hugged her tight, thanking her for her many years of love and company.

The following week I got a series of texts from Jay. My financial aid letter had arrived, pictures of it were in my email. I had been nervous that I had gotten into Georgetown, yet ultimately would be unable to afford it. I stealthily opened my email in the back of my government class. I had never looked at a financial aid award letter before. There were lots of costs all tallied together. The strings of numbers intimidated me. I saw a total hovering in the region of $70,000.

But my panic was succeeded by a rising excitement as I began to decipher what it all meant. I had been awarded a full scholarship to attend Georgetown! Along with my full scholarship came the offer to visit Georgetown for free. I, along with other recipients of the scholarship, were to get an exclusive look at the university.

In January, I found myself on a plane to Washington, D.C., for a week of dinners with Georgetown alumni, members of Congress, and current students. My visit to Georgetown initiated me into the world of fancy dinners and networking. I was expected to dress up and attend a multi-course meal with Georgetown faculty, politicians, and others. The finest attire I had brought with me consisted of dark jeans and a long-sleeved shirt. Others around me were in suits and dresses. I felt out of place but tried not to wear it on my face. I was seated next to a gentleman who turned out to be a congressman on faculty at Georgetown. The version of me who lived on the streets of Tijuana would have never dreamt of being in such a place with such company.

I sat silent most of the meal, puzzling over what would be a worthy conversation topic for such an occasion. I thought back to the movies I had seen depicting gatherings of such a nature. Stocks, classical music, the theater, time-shares, galas . . . I listed stereotypical "fancy" conversation topics in my head only to realize I didn't have much to say on such matters. I watched those around me for signals on which fork and spoon went with which dish. We had a fancy multi-layered, Jell-O-like substance for dessert, another thing I had never encountered before. As I went to stab the dessert, the whole thing ricocheted off the prongs, sliding of my plate and onto the congressman's lap. Mortified, I held my breath as my eyes slowly traveled upward to meet his.

"Ah, I'm so sorry, congressman." I reminded myself to breathe. Inhale. Exhale.

He waved his hand in the air. "It's all right. These things are slippery." He laughed, demonstrating on his own dessert as a bump of his fork set it in motion across his plate.

Still, I hadn't seen anyone else make such a foolish mistake. I could feel my cheeks burning red. The congressman had to assure me three more times that it was all right before I could let it go. I watched as he scooped up dessert from his fresh suit, depositing it into his linen dinner napkin. Once he tidied up, he pulled a business card from the inside of his jacket pocket.

"Here you go. You can contact me should you have any questions about Georgetown." I was shocked that he was still willing to have a conversation with me after I had sullied his expensive suit.

"Okay, thank you, I really appreciate it." I stared down at the thick, embossed business card. It was my first time receiving one, and I didn't know what to do with it. I held it in my hand for the next hour before stowing it away in my pocket.

With this one Georgetown dinner, I began to realize that I had a lot to learn about navigating institutions like Georgetown. My exuberance over having gotten in slowly transformed into a worry about the way I dressed and my lack of knowledge surrounding fine dining and dinner table conversation. Imposter syndrome began to set in.

Soon after, I was receiving more college acceptances to liberal arts colleges along the West and East Coasts. With five more acceptances under my belt, the last thing I was waiting for was to hear back from the Ivies I had applied to. I was especially eager to hear from Brown.

Though I had originally left Brown off of my college list, Jay had insisted that I put it in.

"Hermione from Harry Potter went there! You'd love it," he told me.

Once I began seriously looking into Brown, I did love it. Most appealing to me was the lack of general education requirements. Brown would let me take whatever I wanted so long as I walked away after four years having completed the requirements for a concentration (their version of a major).

Ivy decisions were slotted to come out all at once at 2:00 p.m. on the last day of March. I was sitting in my ceramics class, impatiently counting down the minutes. Too nervous to actually focus on the tile I was carving, I merely sprayed my shaped clay every handful of minutes to keep it from getting too dry. At five minutes to 2:00 p.m., I went to wait in the school bathroom. I needed to be alone.

I locked myself in the furthest stall, and at 2:00 p.m. on the dot, I began checking my decisions on my phone. I received one rejection, then another, and was waitlisted at another. While I was disappointed, I was not surprised. I knew my chances were slim from the get-go.

With all of this in mind, I proceeded to open my last decision. I had saved Brown for last. My fingers were shaking as I typed in my username and password to view my decision. An electronic letter from the admissions office was brought up on my screen. I frantically scanned until my eyes clung to that magic word: "Congratulations."

I tore out of the bathroom and ran through campus. Not knowing what to do with myself, I flopped down on the grass and stared at the blue sky. Breathless, I watched the clouds glide by above me. I realized I hadn't read my financial aid decision, and my celebrating was grounded. Heaving myself into a seated position, I pulled up the letter and once again struggled to navigate the swarm of numbers on the screen.

I had been awarded a full scholarship to Brown on behalf of the Sidney E. Frank Scholars Program! A quick google of Sidney E. Frank revealed a man who had secured the importing rights for Jägermeister in the United States and was the developer of Grey Goose Vodka. I burst into laughter. I thought it was hilarious that my education might be funded by alcohol riches. I thought about Mom and her thermos, how she had filled it with vodka and orange juice to get through her graveyard shifts at the prison. Now alcohol was helping me get through my education.

The hours after my acceptance to Brown were a blur. It felt like the impossible had happened. I was speechless. Many of my friends and teachers came up to me knowing it had been Ivy Day. I told them the good news.

"I'd expect nothing less."

"YES."

"Congratulations, you earned this."

I knew I did not earn it alone. My acceptance was earned by my community. It was made possible by my brother's countless hours spent helping me figure out the application process and the many years that he pushed me to not only catch up in school but to do my best. It was made possible by Teressa forcing me to take breaks with her and relax because no one can accomplish anything when they're burnt out. It was made possible by the countless Inspire teachers who encouraged me to think big and who met with me before and after school to answer my questions on the homework. It was made possible by Justin and Lisa who helped me live in the present and even look forward to the future. It was made possible by my friends whose love, support, and jokes energized me.

Brown offered to fly me out for admitted students' day. Upon my arrival, instead of a fancy dinner, I had been shepherded to a buffet and ate on the grass. I felt at home. That night I accepted my offer to attend Brown come fall.

The night before I left for my first semester at Brown, Teressa helped me condense my belongings into two large suitcases and a backpack. She proved herself to be a master of Tetris and has since been my trusted advisor every time I pack for a long trip. Over one-third of my luggage space was consumed with knickknacks I planned on strewing throughout my dorm room to remind me of home. I had tapestries, string lights, a bamboo mat for my coffee station, mugs and mason jars, stuffed animals, picture frames, and a portable globe. Having moved all around Tijuana with few possessions to my name, I wanted to bring as much as I could carry to my new home in Providence.

I arrived on campus a week before formal orientation began to attend a pre-orientation program that initiated participants into conversations surrounding race, class, sexuality, structural inequalities, and more. I was gaining a whole new language to examine the world around me. It was during this program that I met many of the friends

I was to keep for the next four years, all of them living in the same building as me. There was Emily from New York City whose accent I mistakenly deemed as British (I had never met anyone from New York City before), Laura from Puerto Rico, Daniel and David from Texas, Marianna from my home state of California, and Cole from Connecticut. Never before had I met people from so many different places with so many unique talents and interests.

Yet amid the excitement of all that was new, I was struggling with the transition. Two weeks into living in the dorms, I called my brother and told him I wanted to transfer.

"I'm overwhelmed, Jay," I confessed. "The kids I'm meeting here went to fancy private schools, they have traveled all over the world already, some of them know Latin. I can't compete!"

"Transitions are hard, but I know you can do this. You shouldn't make any decisions about transferring until you finish your first semester."

"I just don't feel like I fit in. I feel like a fraud." I thought about how I had overheard classmates talking about office hours and internships. The thought of going in to sit in a professor's office to talk about the course material and my ambitions made me nauseous. "Plus, people keep asking me what my parents do for a living and who they are ..."

"Oh ..."

"You should see their faces when I try to explain that I don't have contact with my parents and was raised by my older brother and his wife. Some of them then continue on to ask what happened to my parents. It's too much. Why do they even care? Who cares what others' parents do? When I told a stranger about Mom and her addiction the conversation went dead silent until they could find an excuse to walk away."

Jay listened to me patiently as I ranted. Just thinking about another student asking me who my parents were or what they did made me want to break into tears. I felt judged each time, as if my askers were expecting that if I was at Brown, I must be related to someone or come from a certain background.

"Next time someone asks, you just tell them: 'Ah, you wouldn't know them,' and then laugh it off," Jay suggested.

"Yeah, that is a good way to deflect," I admitted. "And get this: there are some kids here who have winter coats more expensive than a brand-new laptop. They're made out of some special Canadian goose."

"Just try and adjust," Jay repeated. "It'll take some time, but you spent quite a lot of time trying to get where you are."

Jay was right. It did take time. I struggled during my first semester and produced what I saw as mediocre papers compared to the rest of my peers. Not accustomed to seeking out help, I avoided office hours and any resources that would have assisted me with my writing outside of class.

I doubled down on my personal efforts. I spent no less than eight hours a day working every day of the week. I read every page assigned to me and exchanged papers with Marianna, a fellow Californian whose room became David's and my desired hangout. Seated on the floor against her desk or alongside each other on the bed, Marianna would provide feedback on some of my writing, and I would do the same for her. I found people like myself who were first-generation and/or low-income, and we talked frankly about our struggles. We acknowledged that we were not starting from the same place academically and professionally as some of our peers, but we were determined to succeed on our own terms.

In this way, I slowly and maturely began to thrive at Brown. I had library mates to keep me accountable for grinding on the weekends and confidants to discuss difficult life things with. I had good friends who knew how to have fun and relax. Laura, Emily, Daniel, and I became inseparable on weekends. We'd crank the music up and dance every Friday without fail, and every Friday, Laura and Daniel would try to teach me how to dance. They are both excellent dancers, and I am not. On Saturday mornings, we'd wake up and get brunch together before heading to the library. While navigating Brown felt impossible on my own, it became very possible with my community of friends alongside me.

Laura, Daniel, Emily, and I had a season when we were obsessed with getting on as many roofs throughout Brown as we could. After checking the easy ones off our list, we set our eyes on a more difficult prize: the roof of a four-story, labyrinthine academic building. Entering the building at around 10:00 p.m., we wandered through endless hallways, our efforts dashed by many locked doors, before we decided to split up. We agreed that whoever made it to the roof would show the others the way. I ran into a member of the cleaning staff who was nice enough to point me in the direction of roof access.

"Students not really supposed to go on roof," she cautioned.

"It's my dream. I have a bucket list . . . Can I go?" She smiled and gave me a slight nod. I set off with her blessing.

The door leading onto the roof indicated that it was alarmed. I knew better. The last five doors had told me the same thing, so I took the risk and pushed it open. No alarm. I smiled as I emerged onto the roof, the night sky above me littered with a few visible stars. Providence had a lot more light pollution than I was used to. I looked down at the sidewalk below. The occasional student strolled by with their backpack, clutching some food; a security guard was stationed right below.

I pulled myself back from the edge of the building, not wanting to get caught. *I should go find the others.* In my excitement of having finally made it onto the roof, the door had swung shut behind me. It was locked from the inside. I was trapped outside, and my phone had 3 percent battery left. I called Laura and hastily explained my situation.

"Lauraaaaa," I cried her name with my classic exaggeration, "Come get me!"

"Okay, we're coming. How do we get there?"

"Ummm . . . There were a lot of turns, some doors I went through . . ." My phone died.

Twenty minutes later, my friends emerged onto the roof to great me. They found me leaning back against the brick wall, enjoying the view over nighttime Providence.

The cleaning staff member had shown them the way, and she emerged onto the roof with them.

"Don't want you to get in trouble," she scolded me, smiling.

I appreciated her commitment to getting me out of this conundrum unscathed. Our dreams of reaching future roofs died with us that night. I didn't want to get anyone in trouble.

No longer sneaking onto roofs, we were in search of a new adventure. Some of us decided to explore the resiliency of Brown's elevators one night after dinner. Laura, Emily, Cole, Marianna, and I entered the elevator on the first floor of our dorm building, headed for the fourth floor. I don't remember who came up with the idea, but all of a sudden, we had all agreed to jump on the count of three. I pushed the idea that we might cause the elevator to come crashing back down to the first floor to the back of my mind in favor of finding out the results of our youthful experiment.

"One ... two ... and three!" we shouted as we jumped with loose synchronicity in the moving elevator. By the time I landed back on my feet, the elevator had come to a grinding halt.

We looked around at each other in silence before breaking out into laughter and commentary. Tightlipped, I shook my head in acknowledgment of our all-too-predictable circumstances before breaking out into a grin.

"Hello? Is anyone there," Laura yelled, trying to get the attention of someone in a dorm hallway.

"Hello?" we heard back. "What's going on?"

"We're stuck!" we responded in chorus. "Maybe you can call the elevator and see if it starts up again?"

No luck. We were stuck in between the third and fourth floors. Our only recourse was to summon help using the red emergency button.

Pressing down the button, we relayed our predicament and location into the speaker. Nothing.

We pulled out our phones to check for a signal. One of our phones had a single bar. Cole held it up high in the corner of the elevator that had signal as we continued to press the red emergency button. Just as we were about to call a friend to get help, a voice on the speaker came through laced with static. "Yes, hello, help is on its way."

"Thank you! We'll be here."

We all slumped to the floor in different corners of the elevator, stretching out our legs as we made ourselves comfortable. I wondered to myself if running out of air was an issue. I wondered what would happen if one of us had to pee. Having watched too many action films, I wondered if one of us could be boosted up through a hidden hatch onto the top of the elevator where they could then pry open the stainless-steel doors revealing the fourth-floor hallway.

The longer we sat in the elevator, the more disappointed conversations we overheard on the third and fourth floors as fellow students tried to summon the elevator.

"Sorry, it's stuck!" we'd shout, alarming hopeful elevator-takers with our hidden presence.

We had been in the elevator for nearly an hour by the time the fire department arrived. Men in loose pants, T-shirts, and suspenders pried open the door and lowered down a ladder. One by one, we crawled up the ladder and onto the carpeted hallway above. After thanking our rescuers, we were let go without questioning. Unfortunately, the elevator was out of commission for the next few days. Remorseful for the hassle we created, we no longer tested the limits of Brown University elevators.

With both rooftop outings and elevator experiments off the table, my recklessly adventurous energy needed to be directed elsewhere. I moved on to sneaking into a closed-off meditation and relaxation outdoor area that sat behind one of Brown's main libraries with Daniel. While the space had previously been accessible via the back of the library, the staff had closed it off since students were taking library books outside and chucking them over the wall to retrieve later. The only way to enter the outdoor enclosure was to shimmy along the edge of the second story of the library and swing one's leg over the high staircase railing.

Daniel bravely led the way the first time, and I followed suit, imagining how ridiculous we appeared to the students inside the library who were watching us through floor-to-ceiling windows. Having survived my first exploratory mission, I returned often to the enclosure to enjoy the company of the possum that could sometimes be found in one of the bushes.

Anyone visiting Brown's campus today will find a sign in our honor warning adventure seekers that cameras are watching and it is advised that you not shimmy along the second story's ledge.

I decided to take a course on the history of captivity and imprisonment my first semester after reading Michelle Alexander's book *The New Jim Crow*. *The New Jim Crow* introduced me to how racism was preserved within and perpetuated by institutions and structures in the present day, including the American criminal justice system.[11]

With my new knowledge of the entrenched racism present within our criminal justice system, I wanted to do something. I signed up to teach GED test prep material at the Rhode Island prison so I could work with incarcerated persons as they studied to get their high school diplomas. I was one of a couple of handfuls of Brown University students who were volunteering a couple of hours a week. I was assigned to medium security and placed in a classroom with a teacher and twenty students. Some students were in their twenties; others were in their forties and fifties.

Immediately, I noticed that at least three out of four students in the classroom were people of color. As I worked one on one with students on reading, writing, and math, they told me their stories. Many of them thanked me for being there. Some of the students I talked to were in there for marijuana possession.

---

11   Michelle Alexander, *The New Jim Crow: Mass Incarceration in the Age of Colorblindness* (New York: New Press, 2012).

I felt sick to my stomach upon hearing this. There wasn't a day that went by when my dorm building didn't smell like marijuana. Brown University students, especially white students, smoked it openly on campus. Marijuana was freely passed around at on-campus parties and sold out of dorm rooms. It was hard to imagine that a Brown University student would ever be arrested on marijuana charges. Yet here were all of these people without high school degrees who were spending time in prison only to exit with the label "felon," which makes it nearly impossible to find employment.[12] I was disgusted by the double standard and the clear indication that the criminal justice system favors incarcerating people of color.[13]

Over the next six months, I saw the right to attend our GED class revoked as the most obvious punishment for poor behavior. Sass a guard? You don't get to attend class for the next week. Get in a fight? No more learning for the next two months.

I had a guard objectify and sexualize me when no one else was around, offering to come into a single-stall bathroom with me after telling me I was beautiful.

I saw an incarcerated person drop to the ground as he was rattled by a seizure caused by intense heroin withdrawal. His attending guard stood laughing as I screamed at him to get help. I pictured my mom on the ground, in pain, as laughs echoed off the concrete walls surrounding her.

---

12   Binyamin Appelbaum, "Out of Trouble, but Criminal Records Keep Men Out of Work," *New York Times*, February 28, 2015.

13   NAACP, "Criminal Justice Fact Sheet," accessed February 28, 2021.

"Help! Help! Someone is hurt!" I yelled. Other guards took their time arriving, strolling casually down the hallway.

"Bastard deserves it," said a voice behind me.

"I'm sorry," I whispered to the man lying on the ground as I held back my tears and rage.

When I returned to the classroom this had happened right outside of, I found that the guard attending the classroom was also making light of the event.

"It's not funny. He's suffering," I spoke through my teeth, my jaw tightly clenched. I noticed some of my students' gazes, a brief flash in their eyes just with my mere acknowledgment of their humanity and dignity.

There is nothing crueler, I decided, than delighting in another's suffering.

The more I learned at Brown and the more I met people from all around the globe, the more I wanted to go and see the world for myself. For the first time in my life, I had the time and the means to do so. I had been saving up money from working part-time as a catering assistant in the basement of one of Brown's dining halls and had also taken out extra loans, banking on the fact that I'd have some sort of decent-paying job in the future.

The summer between my first and second years at Brown, I went to visit Justin and Lisa, who were living in Kenya at the time. My longtime friend Beverly came along as we traveled from San Francisco to Dubai to

Nairobi. I first met Beverly in seventh grade when I began attending youth group. We learned to play the guitar together, we went camping together, and we could always be found laughing together. At our stopover in Dubai, we craned our necks upward at the world's tallest building, the Burj Khalifa, as our long brown hair trailed down our backs. The Burj Khalifa pierced the sky like a grand lightning bolt, seeming to bend space around it with its incomparable height.

In Kenya, we stayed about an hour's drive outside of Nairobi, just a short drive from Nairobi National Park and the local giraffe and elephant orphanages. Justin and Lisa lived in a home encircled by a cinderblock and barbed wire fence. Three dogs greeted me at the gate. I had flashbacks to the compound in Mexico where Mom took me to meet her boss and flinched as the dogs ran toward me. I reminded myself that I was safe, as I often find myself doing.

Justin and Lisa's house was located at the very edge of a canyon. We could hear prayers emanate over a local mosque's speakers as they echoed through the canyon as clear as if they were happening inside our own home. I appreciated the richness of the sounds and how they served to mark the passage of time.

We spent plenty of my five-week stay outdoors. I was in love with the wildlife. Justin and I took many a ride on his motorcycle out into Nairobi Park. Upon glimpsing a gathering of animals, we'd slow the bike to a halt and watch them. Zebra and kudu (antelopes) were the most common. If we went down to the pond near our home, we could spot hippos and fraternize with some cows. Baboons could be spotted along the streets, eyeing their next target and deciding whose groceries they could get away with stealing.

My favorite thing, though, was to go to the elephant orphanage. Every day at around five o'clock, the orphanage workers would bring the baby elephants home from a day out in the park in a grand parade. Trotting single file, elephants would pass by a crowd of onlookers en route to be outfitted with the cozy blankets they often wore across their backs. Back at their pens, each elephant would be given a nighttime bottle of milk that they'd clutch with their trunks and happily gulp down.

One weekend we traveled to Crescent Island—a sort of mini park where all sorts of birds, snakes, and other animals gathered. A small boat trip through hippo-infested waters let us off at the edge of the park, where we were free to walk around among the animals without the threat of predators. Beverly and I stood but five feet away from a giraffe, staring up at its long, slender neck as it grazed on an acacia tree.

"Don't stand right behind it! It can kick you with its hind legs," cautioned Justin.

Beverly and I quickly jogged backwards. I had been so caught up in the wonder of seeing a giraffe up close, I had forgotten to mind its space. I wondered if people survived being kicked by giraffes.

As we explored the park, zebra trotted by right in front of us. I noticed the skulls of antelopes and other animals littering the ground. I had never been so close to all these different types of beings. The lack of boundaries between us was exhilarating. I marveled at how far removed some of us humans, myself included, were from other types of beings, as well as how far removed I felt from the reality of death. I saw some of the first skeletons I'd ever seen that day and had quickly averted my eyes.

After my time in Kenya, I returned for my second year at Brown to room with Marianna, my personal writing coach. We lived one floor below the room where Emma Watson supposedly stayed while she was at Brown. I immediately called Jay to inform him of this great news. I treasured this loose association with Emma Watson as I adored Harry Potter as a kid and still do. It was one of the first series I'd watched through with Teressa, eagerly anticipating the release of each movie in theaters when Teressa and I would pack her purse full of fast food and snacks to feast on while viewing

Like me, Harry grew up without his biological parents and made his own family. Harry also found a safe haven in school, just as I did when I came back to the United States to live with my brother. Hermione, played by Emma Watson, was an intelligent, loyal, and kind friend to Harry. I aspired to be like her growing up. Like Hermione, I wanted to learn not just for the sake of learning but so that I might apply it to help others and to protect and care for my friends. This is all to say it was an incredible feeling to be getting an education one floor below where Emma Watson got hers.

During my first week back at Brown, I saw there was a special course focused on the history and practice of Rinzai Zen Buddhism that had a few spots left. After the semester of in-class meetings and discussions, all course members were funded to spend two weeks studying Rinzai Zen in monasteries throughout Japan! I couldn't believe that Brown was going to pay for students to go to Japan. Though I didn't feel fully qualified, I had to apply. I had already taken a few courses on Buddhism and was interested in learning more about Buddhist concepts of suffering, impermanence, and interconnectedness, as well as Zen-style meditation practice in particular. I knew there was no better way to learn than to be fully immersed in Japan and practicing Zen meditation myself.

I was admitted the following week as the youngest student in the course. I leapt out of my chair and dashed out of my dorm to go and buy a celebratory latte. Caffeinated and hyped to go to Japan, I spent the next couple of hours shopping online for used copies of the ten or so books required for the course. Yet again, I felt very fortunate to have been given an opportunity I never thought I would have.

Some may be under the impression that meditation is easy: just a matter of sitting still, clearing one's mind, and breathing. This couldn't be further from the truth. In particular, Rinzai Zen meditation practice is intense. Traditionally, Rinzai Zen practitioners wake up long before the sun rises to sit, sockless, in an unheated zendo, in a strict posture that is difficult to hold for long periods of time. They continue their day with tea, communal and simple dining, and chores. Meditation sessions may go long into the night only to resume early the next morning.[14]

---

14   Eshin Nishimura and Giei Satō, *Unsui: A Diary of Zen Monastic Life* (Honolulu: University of Hawaii Press, 1983).

While I knew all this in theory, it was entirely different to experience in practice. For three of my class' fourteen days in Japan, we abided by this intensive schedule at a monastery in Kamakura. We ate in silence with other practitioners, we dressed in our Zen practice and work clothes, and we sat until our limbs and backs ached in a drafty *zendo* (meditation hall) in the dead of winter. The first meditation session began just after 5:00 a.m. Stumbling bleary-eyed into the zendo, we would be struck by the alluring smell of green tea that equipped us with both warmth and caffeination to face the hour-long sitting ahead. As the feeling in my toes and legs deadened, my mind became more still, and the passing of time slowed as I strived to exist merely as the coming and going of my breath. The moments when I managed to exist just as breath were few and far between—intrusive thoughts often managed to force their way in. But when those moments did happen, I was at peace.

Sometime in the middle of the second day of our intensive practice, however, I was crashing. I was still jet-lagged from the twelve-hour flight and exhausted from the early mornings that followed our arrival in Japan from Boston Logan Airport. I snuck back to our communal dorm to have a rest where a local practitioner, Tanaka-san, found me eating a Fruit by the Foot I had pulled from my bag. Tanaka-san was tasked with keeping track of the women during our stay and was living in the dorm with us.

"You must meditate," Tanaka-san said with the bit of English she knew.

I knew but a few words in Japanese and needed to get Tanaka-san on board with the idea of my taking a nap. "I must sleep," I said, mimicking lying on my pillow and shutting my eyes.

"No. Meditate," she rebutted.

"Sleep?" I gestured to my pillow again. "One hour?" I implored. She took a minute to think about it. I pulled a second Fruit by the Foot from my bag hoping to win her over with this final offering of goodwill. Tanaka-san grinned wide, stowed the fruit tape in her pocket, and walked out with a nod.

Later that night, Tanaka-san came up to me and showed me the empty wrapper. "Thank you! Thank you!" she said, hands pressed together. I reciprocated her smile and thanked her for allowing me a brief nap. The morning we left the monastery, I left my last Fruit by the Foot in the dorm room for her.

In the hills above Tokyo, we stayed in a monastery complex that also housed an amusement park. The amusement park came as a real shock, as it can't be seen from the front of the monastery itself. It was only when I climbed the hill in front of the monastery that I saw it early one morning: a Ferris wheel, a bungee jump, and various spinning amusements. Leading down the other side of the hill was an elaborate Christmas-themed light display and a small downtown area filled with shops and restaurants. Encountering all of this for the first time on little sleep, I felt as though I had entered some absurdist realm. I questioned if there had been a special ingredient in my morning rice gruel.

After my surprise settled, I came to absolutely adore the oddity of the juxtaposition of the monastery and the amusement park. It was the meeting of two completely different worlds. It reminded me of how shocked I was when I first started at Brown. I hadn't felt like it made sense for someone of my background to be at a place like Brown. I had to convince myself that Brown and I worked together and that we mutually enhanced each other. Just as the amusement park adds fun and levity to the seriousness of meditation practice, the proximity of the monastery serves to remind amusement park goers of the need to contemplate and be still, at least some of the time.

The third monastery we stayed in was in Kyoto. It snowed while we were there, blanketing the curves of the monastery buildings in white. Our first night, we ate at a small, local restaurant manned by one cook who made us a little bit of everything. He poured sake into our green tea and spooned different unlabeled foods onto our plates until we were full, all the while chain-smoking cigarettes over uncovered boiling pots.

"This would not fly with US health codes," my friend joked.

"No kidding," I chuckled, watching to see if any ash from the cigarette landed in the food our chef was preparing for us.

Believe it or not, it was one of the best meals I had during our stay in Japan. Our chef took a group picture of us that he posted on his Instagram page. I still follow him all these years later. With food that good, I respect his less-than-sanitary methods.

Aside from the food and Zen practice, my favorite thing about our stay in Japan were the gardens. The placement of rocks and the moss that grew on them, the shapes painted by raked gravel, the guided shaping of trees and their branches, the gentle trickle of water—all aspects of the gardens were engineered intentionally and with a wealth of meaning behind them.

We visited the famous rock garden at Ryōan-ji to observe its fifteen stones surrounded by raked gravel. Our visit happened to coincide with fresh snowfall. I didn't mind. I had spent hours studying the shape of the garden in books and the placement of the stones. What I hadn't seen before was Ryōan-ji blanketed in snow. On another outing, we bathed in the soft, green glow of the sunlight and bamboo leaves in the Arashiyama Bamboo Forest and shimmied along its frozen path. Some had taken to skating down the icy path. I skated some, but only against my will as I struggled to find traction with my worn Converse. We also had the opportunity to tour an impressive garden that formerly belonged to a wealthy samurai family. During our visit, it seemed like the combative swan that governed the human-made pond was now the one in charge.

The gardens of Japan gave me a sense of peace unlike any other place I had ever experienced. Their beauty promised me healing; their silence promised me the opportunity of self-reflection and contemplation. Walking through the gardens, I was struck by the majesty of plants and trees, butterflies and flowers, water and rocks. While they had always been majestic, it was only when they were displayed in a natural museum that I took pause to notice.

Now, I bring my "Japanese garden" attitude with me everywhere. I take the time to notice the beauty in the weeds in my lawn, in the forests of Northern California, and in sprawling tree roots that upheave city sidewalks. There is beauty all around if only we pause and take the time to look. It is important, I think, that we find beautiful things to wonder and marvel at. When we behold the beautiful, we are healing, or at the very least, balancing out our pain.

When I first told my brother I wanted to study abroad at Oxford, I could barely get the words out of my mouth because of how unlikely it sounded. I had spent the last two years at Brown working through major imposter syndrome. At times, I still felt like I wasn't as talented or as knowledgeable as those around me. I often thought to myself that Brown just accepted me because of my sob story. But I couldn't get Oxford out of my mind. I loved the idea of taking two courses at a time and delving deep into religion, philosophy, and politics. I was in love with the castles and lush English meadows that I'd seen pictures of online. I had to try. I'd never forgive myself if I threw away my shot.

I spent hours crafting my personal statement in the basement of Brown's thirteen-story library one early morning, sipping iced espresso shots laced with caramel drizzle. I submitted my application and tried my best to forget about it during the months that followed. I didn't want to get my hopes up.

Then one afternoon, I opened my email and found my acceptance letter. I had been offered a place to study philosophy and theology at Oxford. I would be at Pembroke College: the place where J. R. R. Tolkien worked on the Lord of the Rings series in his office, where the founder of the Smithsonian Institution studied alongside the founder of the Fulbright Scholarships. How could I be in the company of these giants? I was the kid who missed a few years of school and didn't have a cent to her name to pay for college. I was the kid who lived on the streets of Tijuana, hustling for cash to help Mom buy her supply. Now I was the adult who attends cocktail parties, three-course dinners, and reads old books in castles.

I arrived in England a week before I was permitted to move into my college's dorms. A friend of a friend let me stay in their charming English home. Set in the downtown of a quaint English village a couple of hours' bus ride from Oxford, I spent my first week in England enjoying the most pleasant walks of my life. I loved the mist that hung in the air, the brilliant green grass, and the uneven cobblestone pathways. I ate my meals at a local pub. The sandwiches came with a cold and foamy Guinness that was as delicious as I was told it would be by the Brown University professors who advised me on my year abroad. From the perfectly dim lighting of pubs to the delicately cared for gardens and lichen-covered gravestones to the constant cloud cover and gentle mist to the charming cottage-like facades, I was perfectly at ease with my surroundings.

I went to visit Oxford a few days before I could move into the dorms. I was absolutely enchanted by just how charming the city was. Oxford, I discovered, was a labyrinth of castle-like structures, libraries, storied walls, pubs, meadows, and entertainers. The downtown thoroughfare was always bustling with tourists and entertainers displaying their talents. Instruments bled into one another as I walked through the busiest two blocks. Walking into Pembroke College, I passed through a giant wooden and metal gate nearly three times my height that had a smaller door built into it to allow easy passage. I felt as if I was entering a fortress in which academics were safely cloistered inside, free to think and write and be in community.

My third night in the dorms, we had a formal welcome dinner. This was the first of many "formal" dinners that required us to be outfitted in our college gowns. Undergraduates like me had sleeveless black gowns with two rectangular tassels that dangled behind us. The academic staff of the college had much fancier garments denoting their status. Pembroke College's dining hall is a humbler version of the Great Hall in Harry Potter. Students sit facing each other at long wooden tables under the watchful portraits of historic college officials, alumni, and other elites. At the far end of the hall is an elevated platform where academic staff and college officials eat. For the formal welcome dinner, I was placed among my peers and college instructors who shared similar interests in religion and philosophy. Dinner was served in courses, and wine was freely poured. Intelligent conversation was expected.

I was so nervous my leg began to bounce uncontrollably, shaking the wine glass of the festively robed academic seated next to me. I had never felt so out of place. There were too many forks and spoons in front of me (even more options than there had been at the Georgetown dinner more than two years prior) and because of the length of the table, I could not tell which glasses belonged to me to drink from. I had missed the course on fine dining etiquette that everyone around me seemed to have taken. *They'll see right through me.* One of the instructors at the table began to discuss the quality of our applications. He told one student near me that they had been accepted despite his preferences. *He's coming for me next.* Thankfully, he skipped over me.

Once I started talking to the other students around me, I completely forgot my nerves. We were all so passionate about our studies. I hit it off with Eitan from Massachusetts—we shared a common love for studying religion, we had similar music tastes, and we both enjoyed a good walk. Naturally, we decided to go check out Oxford together after the dinner. We explored the pubs and music scenes down various alleyways and marveled at the architecture. We wandered for hours in our dress clothes. I was so glad to have a friend within my first couple of nights in this strange and wondrous new place.

My courses began almost immediately after I moved into the dorms. Taking two courses at a time, I received a reading list per course every week. Lists would range from ten suggested articles or books to dozens. Along with the reading list, I'd receive a prompt to focus on. Clutching my reading list, I traveled from library to library, walking miles at times, to collect all of the books I needed to write my papers that week in a grand academic scavenger hunt. I was glad that my books were spread out across the entire city. It gave me an opportunity to explore alleyways that would have otherwise gone unexplored and visit the edges of the city.

Nightly communal dinners became a time for my friends to gather and share all that we were learning from the books we read during the mornings and afternoons cooped up in our rooms. We shared nerve-racking moments with our respective tutors, discussed our papers, and laughed at the absurdity of formal dinners and the gowns we had to wear. As our time at Oxford wore on, our dinner group grew. We expanded from three to seven at our peak. Eitan introduced me to Scooty, a fellow visiting student studying history, who joined our dinners. Both of us being from California, Scooty and I hit it off immediately. We shared the same regional slang and affinity for caffeine. I appreciated Scooty's superpower: his ability to bring a smile to everyone, coupled with his deep care for those around him. I couldn't help but feel good when chatting with Scooty.

We spent at least one night a week at a pub, as many of us as could make it. I could always count on Eitan and Scooty for quality company. There are dozens of pubs in Oxford, spreading from the city center outward into removed meadow locations along the River Thames. If we were willing to walk for a bit, we'd go to the pub dubbed the Eagle and Child, the famed watering hole for J. R. R. Tolkien and C. S. Lewis. Or if in the mood to hang about with some tourists, we'd go to the Turf Tavern where Bill Clinton famously did not inhale marijuana and where the Harry Potter cast hung out during their filming in town.

On nights in, I'd lounge on a bench outside or in a friend's room. Asey, a fellow Brown University student, and I could often be found chatting on a bench overlooking the manicured college lawn, venting our complaints, sharing interesting things we were learning about, and swapping childhood stories. Asey shared memories of her life in Singapore. I shared stories of my life in Tijuana and California. Asey was incredibly easy to talk to and a source of great comfort—I told her about parts of my life that I had not told any of my college friends about before—and it felt good. Because of our talks, I decided to share my background more liberally with my friends.

Other nights, I seated myself against the unused fireplace in Rachel's room, talking well into the night. We counseled each other on our dating lives, ate fried food, and watched romantic comedies. Rachel was a visiting student like me, coming from Bryn Mawr in Pennsylvania. She introduced me to scones and clotted cream. When she first asked me to accompany her to get some, I had no idea what to imagine. I recalled a portrait of the Queen, the concept of bread, and some sort of curdled cream.

"It's delicious," promised Rachel.

"Okay, I trust you." I had promised myself that I would try new foods and say "yes" more during my year abroad.

Rachel and I went to an Alice in Wonderland themed café, and my oh my, it was one of the most delicious breakfasts of my life. I was presented with a warm, moist, crumbly pastry in the shape of a biscuit accompanied by a thick, sweet cream. In that moment, I understood why it was a meal fit for the Queen.

The main street in Oxford was always lined with houseless individuals, seeking monetary donations or food. Each time I passed one of them, I couldn't help but recall the days and nights I spent as a kid without a home to go to at night. I could almost still feel the deep chill that sets into one's bones after hours of being outside and the angry clenching of an empty stomach.

Each time I see a houseless person, I recognize that that could have easily been me. I could have gone into foster care in Mexico, never gotten the education I needed, and ended up on the streets. I could have never surfaced from my depression after losing Mom as a kid and been unable to focus on school or a career. I could have turned to substances to escape the heartache and the memories, only to find myself unable to afford rent. Were it not for the care and support of Jay and Teressa and countless other friends and family, it could have easily been me. With so much uncertainty and suffering in life, there is no room to think otherwise.

While I could handle the Oxford workload for the most part, I often found myself overwhelmed by the expectations and the elitism of the institution itself. I didn't feel like the institution was built for me. I lacked the confidence and connections that so many of my peers had. This became very clear to me during a dinner my second week. Sitting at a table of eight including myself, Bill and Hillary Clinton came up in conversation. It was less than a year after Donald Trump had become president, and we were discussing our disappointments. One person pulled up a photo of them with Hillary Clinton on their phone.

"Yeah, I was at a dinner last year for her campaign," chimed another.

"The Clintons know my parents. Here they are over at our house a couple years back." Another picture flashed.

Everyone at the table except for me seemed to have some degree of connection to the Clintons. I marveled at these odds and at the same time felt incredibly out of place. Once I was able to subdue my paralyzing sense of not being in the same circles as my peers, I decided that I would only focus on what I could control: doing my best while I was at Oxford. Though connectionless, I was here along with everyone else, and I was not going to discount myself.

Most of my courses consisted of me presenting my paper's central arguments to my tutor and tackling any questions they threw at me to the best of my ability. During my first term, though, I enrolled in a ten-person graduate seminar on the Danish philosopher and famous existentialist Soren Kierkegaard. Once a week, I'd walk just over a mile from my college at the center of Oxford to Wycliffe Hall, a Church of England theological college. Along the way, I'd rehearse the key points I had taken away from the book assigned to us that week, my contemplation frequently broken by the happenings of the bustling city around me. I felt lucky to be included in the course since I was neither a graduate student nor an advanced theology student. I did, however, come to the course with a deep commitment to learning about Kierkegaard's life and philosophy. Ever since I had read *Fear and Trembling* by him my first year at Brown, I felt an unexpected bond with and affinity for Kierkegaard, even though we were separated by nearly two centuries. Kierkegaard, I knew, had much to teach me about my own mortality, purpose for living, and how to believe the seemingly impossible will be made possible.

Kierkegaard often amused himself by walking around his hometown people-watching. He loved to read, felt compelled to write, and believed that the academics around him should be judged by their actions rather than their intellectual artifacts.[15] We share these things in common.

Kierkegaard grew up convinced that he was going to die before he reached the age of thirty-four.[16] He inherited this conviction from his father, who, out of a place of deep religious guilt, was convinced that all seven of his children were destined to die before they reached Jesus' age when he was crucified.[17] Internalizing the brevity of his life, Kierkegaard worked fiercely and deliberately.

Five of Kierkegaard's siblings died before the age of thirty-four.[18] But Kierkegaard and his older brother survived. Kierkegaard was so surprised when he lived past his thirty-fourth birthday that he checked the parish records to make sure that he had gotten his birthday right; he was indeed thirty-four years old.

Although I've never been told when I will die, I existed for many of my teenage years with a debilitating fear of my mortality and the belief that I would inevitably die young. Having survived drowning on the eve of my move to Mexico and pneumonia in a Tijuana hotel, I spent

---

15   Alastair Hannay, *Kierkegaard: A Biography* (Cambridge: Cambridge University Press, 2001).

16   Ibid, 278.

17   Ibid, 122-123.

18   Ibid, 31-33.

many nights of my youth thinking of how I would die. The absolute impermanence of everything around me did not permit me to rest most nights. Just as I lost Mom, I thought about how I would eventually lose everyone else that I loved. These thoughts plagued me throughout most of high school, and when I did manage to sleep, I often dreamt of the moments leading up to my last breath.

Some nights, I would be transported back to the compound in Tijuana, watching a gun be drawn from the waistband of Levi's. Other nights, I'd be driving along with my brother, and all of a sudden, we would be weightless as we plummeted into the canyon below us. Afterward, I would wake up in my bed, sweating and calling out for help.

Plagued by my mortality, I signed up for afternoon and evening courses on religion at Chico State University that I attended after high school let out. I found comfort in the many ways that different traditions and individuals conceptualized mortality and impermanence. Change and death are the two most sure things in life. I say change and not taxes because, well, just look at how the ultra-rich in America manage to get away with not paying theirs.

Around the same time I began to study religion, I was introduced to the philosopher and writer Henry David Thoreau. Living in Massachusetts in the 1800s, Thoreau embarked on a two-year experiment as he approached the age of thirty. He moved into a sparsely furnished cabin in the woods along Walden Pond in Concord, Massachusetts. There in this cabin, he began his experiment on simple living: tending his vegetable patch, observing the plurality of creatures around him, and thinking.[19] Living just on the outskirts of town, he had the distance he needed for deep spiritual, personal, and societal reflection.

Thoreau recounted his experiences in his book *Walden, Or Life in the Woods*. In my favorite section of *Walden*, Thoreau writes:

> "I went to the woods because I wished to live deliberately, to front only the essential facts of life, and see if I could not learn what it had to teach, and not, when I came to die, discover that I had not lived . . . I wanted to live deep and suck out all the marrow of life, to live so sturdily and Spartan-like as to put to rout all that was not life . . ."[20]

Reading this passage in my morning high school English class, I suddenly became deeply aware of my mortality in a new and oddly invigorating way. From Thoreau's words, I glimpsed someone who knew that the real dilemma was not the fact of one's mortality, but rather how one lives when they have a finite amount of time left on this Earth. Thoreau withdrew to his cabin to sort out for himself what living meant for him. Ever since I read these words, I have been trying to do the same.

I went to visit Walden Pond in my second year at Brown. The first thing I noticed was the rich color palette of the fall leaves and how if one briefly glanced it would be difficult to tell the difference between the sky and

---

19 Henry David Thoreau, *Walden and Civil Disobedience* (Digireads.com, 2013).

20 Ibid, 1246.

the water's reflection of it. On my visit, I met a Harvard botany professor who introduced me to some of the local flora and fauna. Crawling on his hands and knees, he beckoned me down for a closer look at the life around me.

"You have got to see this!" the professor exclaimed as I lowered myself to my knees on the ground beside him. "Isn't it beautiful?"

"They really are," I replied, admiring the delicate purple flowers to which he had directed my attention.

Just weeks before my visit to Walden Pond, a classmate of mine had said, "You don't need the perfect mountaintop to appreciate beauty."

I recalled this wisdom as I knelt on the ground next to the professor, dreaming of other ways that beauty can be appreciated and feeling thankful I was learning a new one. I was moved by how captivated the professor was by these plants sprouting from the ground, and I found myself yet again wondering what I found important enough to center my life around. *Where do I find beauty? Where do I find meaning?* Standing next to the marked area where Thoreau's cabin had stood, I tried to visualize what it would be like to undertake such a prolonged period of self-reflection.

Like Thoreau, I am in a state of withdrawal from society. As I write this in October of 2020, I am in my sixth month of living at home with Jay and Teressa waiting out the coronavirus pandemic. I leave for brief trips to the grocery store, but otherwise, I sit in my small space writing and working, enjoying the vegetables Jay and Teressa have grown, and reflecting. COVID has forced me to pare down my life to its most essential facts; it has left me with few distractions. This transition from constant work to simple living has been jarring, even painful. But it has served to more fully illuminate for myself how I can best live deeply. I have realized that a deliberate life for me is spent contributing to conversations and formulating solutions around the issues of poverty, addiction, and climate change.

The magnitude and severity of these issues is daunting. With problems this large, most of our natural inclinations, including mine, are to resign ourselves to the fact of their existence and fall into despair or apathy. Change in these areas often feels impossible given, for example, the severity of the stigma surrounding poverty and addiction and the resistance of industries and policymakers to enact substantial reforms in response to climate change. I have found that these issues become approachable when I do so with a leap of faith.

Kierkegaard first came up with the term "leap of faith" as a metaphor for faith in God. In *Fear and Trembling*, Kierkegaard reflects on the passage in Genesis in which God commands Abraham to sacrifice his son, Isaac.[21] How could an ethical God ask a father to murder his son? And how could someone willing to murder their son be lauded as a hero of faith?[22] Kierkegaard navigates the paradox of an ethical God commanding a father to murder his son and a father believing the sacrifice to be a holy act by developing the concept of a leap of faith.[23]

Abraham's leap of faith was his willingness to sacrifice his son with the belief that he would get Isaac back in this lifetime. Even though Abraham couldn't rationally

---

21 Søren Kierkegaard, *Fear and Trembling* (A&D Books, 2014).

22 Ibid, 22.

23 Ibid, 74-75.

justify why he was making the seemingly unethical decision to sacrifice Isaac, he had faith that Isaac would somehow return to him.[24] So Abraham arrived at Mount Moriah where he was told by God to make the sacrifice, he bound Isaac, and just as he began to lower the knife, God stopped him and provided an alternate sacrifice in the form of a ram caught in a thicket.[25]

Separating the concept of a leap of faith from its Christian context, we might think of Kierkegaard's leap of faith as a movement that occurs when one reaches the limits of reason and decides to believe in a particular outcome anyway, even when the outcome does not seem possible. When Jay believed I could catch up on years of missed school in a couple of months, he took a leap of faith; I leapt when I believed that I could win my district spelling bee my first year back in school.

To take a leap of faith is to be willing to imagine radical alternatives to the present moment despite significant barriers to its realization. A leap of faith acknowledges that the way we think about and approach our greatest problems is able to be otherwise no matter how entrenched certain attitudes and policies may appear.

Believing in the possibility of change is sufficient justification for continuing to take on problems as daunting as poverty, addiction, and climate change. Imagined alternatives will become real solutions when enough of us take the leap and believe such changes to be possible.

---

24 Ibid, 27.

25 Genesis 22: 1-19 (NIV).

There were never any dull moments during my year at Oxford. I either felt like I was in a pressure cooker, determined to impress my tutors and succeed no matter the cost to my personal health, or I was on top of the world, enchanted by the scenery and opportunities that surrounded me. I saw Oxford and Brown as my chances to literally write my way into a new life, into more opportunities and financial security. I approached each paper with a deep seriousness, as if each good paper would earn me a fraction of a ticket to a life secure from poverty.

Working hard became my defining trait. I worked hard even when I knew I needed to rest. I was addicted to the promise of reward. This is not to say I didn't work hard for other reasons. I sincerely felt that everything I was thinking and writing about was important and deserving of careful reflection. I just didn't know how to dial my investment back. Hard work had become my life raft and a defensive tool I employed to refrain from dealing with the baggage that was dragging me down.

I am embarrassed to admit that I have sought solace in work during the most heartbreaking moments of my life. When I arrived at Oxford, I didn't give myself time to reflect on all that had happened with Mom.

During the summer before Oxford, an unknown number flashed across my screen, its structure signaling to me that it came from outside the country. It was Alex. It was our first time talking in over a decade, and I scarcely recognized his voice as he asked me for money.

"Your Mom is sick—very sick," I heard. I was frozen, silent, and still. I had up to that point been convinced that Mom had been dead for years. She had our phone numbers; she could have called, but she never did.

"What's wrong?" I heard myself ask. My voice sounded strange to me.

"She's had some, um, complications from her pregnancy . . ." Alex trailed off.

"Pregnancy?"

"I have a son," Alex said, his voice laden with emotion. He had always wanted a son. I tried to process the fact that I had another half brother.

Mom had had a third child at the age of fifty-eight. Years of hard drug use and going through a pregnancy at her age had left her in a bad state. She was being cared for in a hospital in Guadalajara, Mexico, southeast of where we had lived together in Tijuana.

"I have to talk to her. I have to talk to Mom," I blurted out, forgetting to ask the name of Alex's son.

Mom didn't know Alex was calling me, and I was informed that she would be angry if she did. Alex was calling to see if Jay and I might help with some of her medical bills. We pooled some money together and wired it via Western Union. In turn, I made Alex promise that he'd get Mom on the phone.

When I received Alex's call, I had been staying in Providence for a couple of weeks visiting friends before my move to England. Alex told me he'd try to get Mom on the phone, so I sat next to my phone for days on end in Marianna's living room. Every call placed to Alex went to voicemail. I stayed up late, terrified that I would fall asleep and miss a call from Mom.

By the fourth day, I was in agony. I walked for miles on end, phone in hand, dripping with sweat in humid Providence. I crumpled onto the lawn of a local school and began calling Alex. I was determined to call him as many times as I needed in order to get ahold of Mom. I promised Jay I would try my best to talk to her. When I finally got ahold of Alex, it took over an hour of pleading for him to finally walk the phone to Mom's bedside.

"Hello, this is your mother," I heard a foreign voice rasp. I realized I had no longer remembered what Mom's voice sounded like. I felt a pang of sorrow that I pushed away so I could focus on the moment.

"Mom! Mom, it's so good to hear your voice. I've really missed you . . . Are you okay? What's wrong? I'm in college right now." I cut myself off, needing to hear her voice again. There was so much I wanted to say—years of my life I wanted to condense into seconds.

But she was gone. Alex was back on the line. He told me she didn't want to talk any more. Alex placed the phone in a doctor's hand who explained that things were not looking good for her. The line went dead.

Alex didn't pick up any of my calls going forward. I felt as if a gaping hole had been punched in my chest. Just like when I was a kid, I lay in bed with my arms crossed tightly across my chest, hoping I'd be able to keep myself from unraveling. I stumbled around Providence for the next few days in shock, numb to what had happened. Drinking iced coffees, I sat in the library and did all of my preparatory readings for Oxford. Nothing felt real, but somehow my body and mind were going through the motions of my life as a student.

I called Jay to tell him the news, holding back tears in the library lobby. I could hear the disappointment in his pauses and his deep breaths.

"I tried my best. She doesn't want to talk to us. She's very sick." I could only manage to speak in short, matter-of-fact sentences.

"Okay . . . That's disappointing."

"Yeah, really disappointing."

Mom had rejected me on her deathbed. She blamed me for leaving and didn't care what I had done with the last decade of my life. Not knowing what to do with the anger that welled inside me, I pounded the wall of the library bathroom before breaking into tears. *Maybe if I had said something different, she would have talked to me.* My head swam with what-ifs. I clung to my hope that she would change her mind and call Jay before it was too late. She never did.

A couple of weeks after I heard Mom's voice, I boarded a plane to London Heathrow. My move to Oxford was bittersweet. Though I was very excited to spend a year studying what I loved in a beautiful place, I was struggling with leaving the country so soon after I learned that Mom was alive but dying. My phone plan wasn't going to work while I was abroad—it was too expensive to keep my number active.

Part of me wanted to hold out hope that she would change her mind and call me back, confessing how much she had missed Jay and me over the last decade, how she wished things would have been different. But I recognized that such a hope was dangerous. Mom called me on my tenth birthday angry that I had abandoned her, and a decade later, she still felt the same way. People feel how they feel whether we agree with it or not. Sometimes how someone feels is just disappointing.

It was only about two months into my time at Oxford that I started to internalize what had happened over the summer with Mom.

I had spent my first term at Oxford trying to write a new me into existence as I buried myself in old books and devoted myself to crafting my weekly papers, but I had come to realize the futility of such an exercise. The emotions that I had buried excavated themselves and began to drown me. *She's sick and dying yet doesn't want to see me. She doesn't give a **** about what I've accomplished. She hates me for leaving her.* These thoughts cycled endlessly; I couldn't focus or write. I could barely even talk. Eventually, I was able to drag myself from my bed. A staff member recommended I see the Pembroke College Chaplain, Andrew Teal.

I arrived at Andrew's office at dusk. Furnished with a couch and two armchairs, his office had a nice view of the lawn, his windowsill lined with carefully selected flowers. One wall was obscured with bookshelves, and stacks of books and papers were sprinkled sporadically throughout the rest of the room. My hands were shaking as I entered the room, my eyes nervously filing away the details of his office.

"Would you like a hot cup of coffee or tea?" Andrew asked me.

"Coffee, please." I was starting to feel comfortable.

I sat down on the couch across from Andrew.

"I'm sorry to hear about your mother," I heard. Andrew's voice was gentle, saturated with kindness. I hadn't received that sort of warmth in a long time, and I forced back the tears that began to well. I nodded vigorously, avoiding eye contact. If I made eye contact, I knew I would be forced to inhabit the moment, and I'd break down.

"I'm sorry, too. I haven't been doing too well," I admitted. "Will this be weird since you're my tutor next term?" I was worried of being too vulnerable with a person that was scheduled to be my instructor on mysticism in just a few short weeks.

"Not weird at all." With this acknowledgment, I relaxed further.

I explained what had happened with Mom before coming to Oxford. The tears began almost instantly, but they were the sort that I could talk through, so I kept going. It was all spilling out: the hurt of her rejection, my sorrow over her suffering, my unreciprocated love for her, the agony of losing her for a second time. Andrew listened to me patiently, nodding, radiating kindness in my direction as tears dripped into my coffee and I piled up used tissues on my lap.

"What do you need to do for yourself in the short-term to handle this?" Andrew asked me.

We decided that I would start prioritizing taking care of myself by being gentle with how much I demanded from myself and being honest about how I was doing. My first step in facing the reality of the situation was to let some of my friends at Oxford know what had happened and to let myself sit with the pain instead of burying it. It was the end of my first term at Oxford, so I flew back home to be with Jay and Teressa for a couple of weeks before beginning a few weeks of traveling.

Returning to Europe after spending some time at home, I was feeling more grounded. Though still grieving, I had made some peace with what happened with Mom and was fully ready to soak up the perks of being abroad, which included ample time to travel across Europe and cheap travel between countries. I began my travels by meeting my friend Emily from Brown in Amsterdam. Mom came with me in spirit. I couldn't get her off of my mind.

Emily and I were staying in a youth-friendly hostel in the center of the city alongside the canals. Amsterdam was beyond charming. Rows of bicycles lined the canal railings, and even more bikes rushed by us as we strolled the shop-lined streets. I was particularly enthused by the cheese shops that provided endless cubed samples and the many cafes littered throughout the city. I appreciated how the labyrinthine web of canals broke up the density of the city. The constant presence of water brought with it a sense that I was never too deep in the concrete jungle that I'd be lost or swept away by a crowd. We spent Christmas Day in our room, watching *America's Next Top Model* and eating Indian food.

I was fascinated by Amsterdam's legalization of prostitution. In the Red Light District, women stand in window displays beckoning clients. These women are equipped with a button to call for help should they feel unsafe in any given encounter with a client.[26] Such a system was a world away from what I had experienced with Mom on the streets of Tijuana. I had feared for her safety when she went away with her client into a hotel room. No one had been looking out for her.

From Amsterdam we moved to Prague. In the town square's Christmas market, we sampled mulled wines, hot ciders, and local edible specialties. A great big tree stood in the center of the market, horses and carriages milling around it. Emily and I celebrated New Year's Eve on the top of a hill we had hiked up behind our Airbnb. Strangers celebrated around us, twirling sparklers, shouting, and laughing. At the top of the hill, we were surrounded by nearly a dozen different fireworks shows occurring across the city. I found myself slowly spinning in circles, trying to take it all in, mesmerized by the

26 "10 Amsterdam Red Light District Safety Measures," Red Light District Tours, November 7, 2017.

booms that rang out all around me and the dazzling lights that filled the sky's canvas.

I was transported back to the neighborhood firework shows I had watched with Mom on New Year's Eve one year in Tijuana. All around us, our neighbors had set off fireworks they had purchased from their enclosed yards. There was clearly a competitive edge to the occasion, as our neighbors responded to other neighbors' fireworks with their own grander series of fireworks. Neighbors battled each other in the sky, explosions of light and sound shaking our metal gates. Mom and I had cheered aloud for our favorites, clapping into the night.

In Vienna, Emily and I attended the opera for the equivalent of ten dollars each. For that low price, we had committed to stand for the entirety of the show in the very back of the theater. The opera was in German; a small screen in front of us showed English subtitles. I found it too difficult to both read and watch, so I opted to just watch. I think I understood about 30 percent of the show. It was all right. The highlight happened during intermission when I glimpsed a young boy, no more than eight years old, outfitted in a full tuxedo—top hat included—carrying a walking stick. Emily and I stopped dead in our tracks to gape at this fancy child. Once I got over the absurdity of the child's dress, I began to feel like we weren't all that different from each other. We both had rather atypical childhoods: his spent attending operas, mine selling my belongings on Tijuana streets.

My favorite part of Vienna ended up being the cafes. Unlike the dark, smoke-filled cafes of Amsterdam, Viennese cafes were palatial. Outfitted with chandeliers, woven carpets, and plush couches and armchairs, Viennese cafes made me feel like royalty each time I sat down. Ordering a cappuccino and a chocolate torte, I spent many hours lounging with a book and soaking up the luxury of the cafe environment during our handful of days in the city. I couldn't help but recall the last time that I had enjoyed such luxury—I was eight years old in the mansion that was lent to Mom and me to rest and prepare for her first assignment as a coyote. Like then, this luxury was not my own but borrowed.

Our last stop before I headed back to Oxford was Budapest. Emily and I visited a cave church on a hill above the Danube River. Formally constructed in the 1920s by a group of Catholic monks, the caves were used as a chapel and monastery until 1951 when they were raided as part of state actions against the Catholic Church. Reopened in 1989, the cave remains in use by Catholic monks in addition to being a prominent tourist attraction.[27]

When Emily and I visited, we found ourselves being led deeper into the rock's core by an intricate system of passageways. We eventually emerged into the inner room where services are held. Scattered flower-filled vases occupied hollowed-out nooks in the rock wall; plastic folding chairs were set up for those who wanted to sit and pray or appreciate the various hand-carved wooden objects decorating the sanctuary. Ducking through low, carved doorways, I tried to imagine living

27 "Budapest Cave Church," Atlas Obscura, accessed March 1, 2021.

within these hollowed-out spaces, the coolness of rock surrounding me on all sides. All I could imagine was what it had felt like during those nearly two days in jail with only a cool concrete slab to rest on. Shivering, I eagerly emerged into the Budapest sun. Though the space evoked claustrophobia and desperation for me, I knew that for others this space had meant safety and protection.

One night in Budapest, Emily and I found ourselves on the Chain Bridge over the River Danube at dusk. We stood admiring the Hungarian parliament building's illumination. We heaved ourselves up on the platform that slowly swept upward to meet the stone arch that cars traveled through below. A third of the way to the arch, the platform had a metal gate—locked—to keep anyone from climbing up too high. We found ourselves climbing up to meet the gate, slowly edging ourselves up above the cars below, our shoes gripping the circular speed bumps put in place so people like us didn't enjoy a fun slide down the platform. The sky was completely dark by the time we had scrambled up. Like the firework-surrounded hill in Prague, I enjoyed this new perspective of the city around me. I watched the lights of illuminated buildings and storefronts dancing on the water below.

After Budapest, I parted ways with Emily as I headed back to Oxford. Eitan and I were taking a course on mysticism with Chaplain Teal. A couple of days before our course began, we received an email inquiring whether it'd be all right to allow Sister Helen, a member of a local convent, to join our conversations. I hurriedly replied with a resounding yes. It's not every day you get to study mysticism with a nun and a chaplain, and I was thrilled at the opportunity to get more perspectives in the conversations.

For the next eight weeks, we all met in Andrew's office. Eitan and I sat on the couch, Andrew and Sister Helen sat in the chairs across from us. We discussed descriptions of mystical experiences had by individuals across different religious traditions and beyond. We discussed poems, books, and films that touched on or described the mystical. We talked about the limits of talking about that which evades being captured in language. All the while, we developed one of the finest learning communities that I've ever been a part of.

When not in class, I found myself mesmerized by YouTube videos of marble runs. I appreciated the intricate courses people had designed in their homes, yards, or elsewhere outdoors, all for the purpose of racing marbles. I rooted for my favorites and appreciated the colors streaking across the screen like running paint. I marveled at the dedication of the people who had painstakingly constructed these courses just because they loved marbles.

I began thinking more about what it meant to do something just for the enjoyment of doing it. Like those who build intricate marble runs simply because they love marbles, I began to do things just for enjoyment's sake. I took three-hour walks through meadows with friends and read a stack of books that was not assigned to me, and I practiced not feeling guilty. I refused to feel like I was falling behind because I was taking a break. While I had had glimpses of an existence focused on enjoying the moment in the past, I had never inhabited the state of being for such a prolonged amount of time. I had predominantly been in survival mode since I was a young kid in Tijuana.

Even though I spent less time working and more time enjoying myself, oddly enough, I was doing better than I had ever done. The quality of my papers improved along with the quality of my life. I saw that the gift of being able to inhabit the present moment outside a capitalist framework of productivity is invaluable. In taking the time to appreciate the beauty around me and to do activities for enjoyment's sake, I had regained my ability to heal. I had learned how to live—not just survive—with the pain of losing Mom.

Alongside mysticism, I took a course on the philosophy of religion. My tutor was a devout atheist with an attention to detail. Each week, I'd enter a dimly lit room to find him waiting at a conference table with a copy of my marked-up paper in hand. The room was always too cold, too drafty. The old stained-glass windows of the room did not properly shut, and there was no central heating, only an unused fireplace.

Seated across from my tutor, I'd read my paper out loud, line by line. Every sentence, or at most every third sentence, he would interrupt me to either critique a part of my argument or to probe me to go deeper.

"Wrong! That's not what Descartes meant by that."

"What do you even mean by that?"

"I don't have a clue as to what you're arguing for."

At our first meeting, the interruptions greatly unnerved me. My arguments were being torn apart in front of my eyes. All of the gaps in my understanding were laid bare.

The second week, I downed a couple of straight espresso shots and walked into the damp room with as much confidence as I could muster. From my first encounter, I had learned that I had to be more assertive and not give in so easily. I acknowledged the soft spots in my argument at the onset and then began to push back, countering his points with well-thought-out responses and firing back with my own questions. He nodded his head in approval.

While I learned to fake my confidence and assert a strong argument, deep down I didn't feel like I had solved any of the questions I was answering. One week, I was tasked with determining whether the Buddhist concept of karma held up to scrutiny; another week I was asked if it would make sense if all religions were true. I learned to build these elaborate arguments and defend them on the surface, yet I only grew increasingly confused on the inside. I initially began studying religion and philosophy to get hard-and-fast answers, but, in the course of my studies, I came to realize the impossibility of such a pursuit—at least for me. While my tutor had gone down a similar path and emerged as a stout atheist with a mission to debunk religion, I only wanted to explore the beautiful diversity of thought out there.

I did not want to tear down or disprove anyone's way of navigating and making sense of this world. Such an act not only felt arrogant but also violent. Who was I to tell someone that the way they made sense of their existence was logically flawed? And even if I did have the credibility to tell someone just that, why would I want to rattle the foundation of their life like that? Mom had found comfort in the Pentecostal Church, and Jay and I had found a home away from home in Christian youth groups at different parts of our lives. I studied religion so that I could stand back and appreciate the ways that communities had learned to navigate suffering and impermanence. I wanted to learn what others thought about our strange circumstances on this rock spinning in a vacuum and how they infused their lives with meaning and beauty.

I wanted to dig deep into the political visions offered by members of different religious traditions. Instead of proving the beliefs of any particular tradition, I was interested in the ways that beliefs, scriptures, and practices were harnessed by members of religious traditions to support social and political activism. How have Buddhists applied the *dharma* (the teachings of the Buddha) to promote human relationships with the environment that acknowledge the reality of interdependence? How have Christian thinkers drawn on scripture to condemn capitalism's desecration of the Earth through its endless mining of resources? What do Jains' deep commitment to *ahimsa* (non-violence against all living things) look like when acted out in a world filled with so much violence against people, animals, and plants—much of which we never know about?

In asking these questions, I was on a quest to learn about the ways that individuals' faith and adherence to a particular set of shared spiritual ideas shaped and deepened the way they engaged with the scientific reality of climate change. I wanted to know how individuals' religious traditions helped them process the existential threat that is climate change, as well as how their traditions prepared them to understand

and engage with the reality of climate change in their own lives. Knowing that the problem of climate change requires a majority of humanity to be committed to finding and implementing solutions, I was trying to understand different perspectives on climate change in order to get an idea of what it might be like to mobilize individuals with a plurality of worldviews to address the issue together. How does a community made up of many communities come together to take on an issue as daunting as climate change?

I carried this question and many others with me as I headed off to Italy with Teressa and her niece Lindsey during my next break at Oxford. Teressa and Lindsey had both flown all the way from California to visit me. I was thankful for the feeling of home that they brought with them, as well as my favorite snacks that Teressa unloaded from her bag onto my bed. A pile of Scooby-Doo gummy snacks brought me back to Mom's and my apartment in Murrieta Hot Springs before we moved to Tijuana. When Mom had extra money, she would buy me a big box of Scooby-Doo gummy snacks that I would eagerly munch down while watching the same *Scooby-Doo* episodes on VHS for the hundredth time.

Teressa, Lindsey, and I visited the Colosseum in the pouring rain. Huddled under an arch, the wind threatened to yank my umbrella from my arms. I felt uneasy standing in a place that had witnessed so much violence and cruelty. I couldn't help but visualize the gathering rain puddles as puddles of blood draining from the slain. *How could so many delight in such violence? How could such acts hold entertainment value?* Thunder crackled from the sky, recalling the crowds who screamed in delight at the sight of defeat and triumph in the blood-soaked ring below. I once again recalled the prison guard who delighted in the sight of someone suffering from a withdrawal-caused seizure.

The next day we toured the Vatican. We were greeted by cardboard cutouts of Pope Francis when we first entered, and video footage of the Pope waving at crowds from the popemobile cycled on a loop. We came during a low tourist tide, so when we arrived at the Sistine Chapel, there were only a few scattered groups present. I reclined on the benches that wrapped around the back of the Chapel, enjoying the easy viewing of the intricate frescoes above. I tried my hand at identifying some of the 343 figures depicted on the ceiling, wondering at the dedication that was required to bring the Old Testament to life. My neck had hurt from a few minutes of gazing upward, and I could not imagine the years Michelangelo spent doing so.[28] My musings were soon interrupted by a guard.

"You should not be lying down, get up. No one can sit if you take up the bench," he said gruffly.

I sat up and peered around me. No one was around me. "I promise I will move if someone comes."

"No, you have to get up," he commanded. "Now."

I wondered what it was like for the guard to spend years of his life working below the ceiling; I wondered if he still even noticed it above him. Sassily, I wondered why it was against etiquette to appreciate the ceiling of the Sistine Chapel while lying on one's back.

---

28   "Sistine Chapel," Musei Vaticani, accessed March 1, 2021.

Leaving Rome, a train transported us three hours across the Italian countryside to deliver us in the center of Venice. Stepping outside the station, we were confronted by the Grand Canal—its picturesque surface dotted with gondolas and water buses.

Venice is a maze of stone alleyways and colored buildings. While crowds gather along the Grand Canal walkway and in Saint Mark's Square with the pigeons, crowds can easily be escaped by darting down the nearest alleyway. One of my favorite things about Venice is the ability to escape into solitude and meander sporadically through the city among the weather-worn buildings. Teressa, Lindsey, and I wandered the backroads of Venice, delighting in the fresh flowers adorning windowsills and feeling a peacefulness that can only be attributed to the complete absence of cars. Venice, we found, is a place built for wanderers without a destination.

On our walks in Venice, I was reminded of one of my favorite reflections from Olivia Laing's *The Lonely City*. In it, Laing writes of those who walk aimlessly and treat walking "not as a means but as an end, an ideal occupation in and of itself."[29] It is somewhat of a revolutionary idea in this age dominated by frantic rushing-about, but I agree with Laing and others that walking is an art unto itself to be enjoyed for its own sake and with no other goal in mind. To walk without a destination is to exist in a richly sacred manner akin, perhaps, to breathing.

Ever since I was a kid in Tijuana, I have enjoyed wandering streets and alleyways, seeing what curiosities

---

29   Olivia Laing, *The Lonely City* (Edinburgh: Canongate Books Ltd., 2016), 156.

are waiting to be discovered. If I am not able to walk about, I am not very happy. I want to be where the people and the trees and the animals are. Like Annie Dillard writes in *Pilgrim at Tinker Creek*, every time I return from observing life outside of my house's walls, "I walk home exhilarated or becalmed, but always changed, alive."[30]

In Venice, I was also drawn to the way buildings bear the mark of environmental time. Those buildings at the water's edge reveal varying waterlines imprinted on their surfaces. The waterside buildings' facades grow ever more faded the lower you look. Algae and other growths have grafted themselves onto homes and storefronts. Water levels threaten to rise even further in the coming years. In 2019, the mayor of Venice, Luigi Brugnaro, attributed the disastrous floods of that year to climate change.[31] While some may hesitate to apply that accusation, it is important to note that five of the ten record-setting floods have occurred in the last twenty years.[32] As devastating Venetian floods occur more frequently, Venetian buildings will record the rising waterlines on their facades.

On the plane ride back to London, I could not shake the image of the beautiful Venetian buildings being overcome by rising sea levels. *Much more than buildings will be lost.* I began to imagine the loss of life, the loss of entire species, the loss of entire islands, of countless homes that would come about as a result of climate change. I felt myself

---

30   Annie Dillard, *Pilgrim at Tinker Creek* (London: HarperCollins Publishers Ltd., 2007), 226.

31   Nikki Berry, "Venice Floods: Climate Change behind Highest Tide in 50 Years, Says Mayor," *BBC*, November 13, 2019.

32   Ibid.

grieving for all that had been lost already and all that I knew would be lost. All I knew then and all I know now is that community is key. It is in community that we will grieve our losses, and it is in community that we have our only hope of acting to prevent further loss.

When at Oxford, my favorite thing to do—narrowly beating out a visit to see the dinosaurs at the Museum of Natural History—was a walk in Port Meadow. Port Meadow is a lush meadow that is intercepted by the River Thames, filled with tall grass, and scattered with flowers. It lies only a mile's walk from the center of Oxford yet feels an eternity away from the deadlines and scholar-packed libraries of the city. Charming wooden bridges allow pedestrians to cross from one side to another. Hiking trails meander through the dense thicket of trees that encircle the meadow. Depending on the day I visited, I would either glimpse free-roaming cows or galloping horses shaking their heads in the breeze. I found myself startled at times by our proximity to each other. I had never shared a common space with cows or horses. I felt the same sort of thrill that I had felt nearly two years ago in Kenya as I walked with the giraffes and zebras.

Crossing over the bridge, I would eye the small boats tethered to the dock and the geese floating on the River Thames below. I often found myself in the company of Eitan, and at times, our friend Scooty, another student from Massachusetts studying abroad at Oxford, following the tree canopy tunnel that led back toward The Perch.

The Perch, a pub with an outdoor garden area, feels as if it has emerged straight from a storybook. A white building complete with crisp black trim and a thatch roof, The Perch sits in the middle of the meadow.

The garden area boasts the largest weeping willow tree I've ever had the pleasure of encountering. Its sheer size and the way its branches elongate downward in a thick stream recall the rushing water of a waterfall. I found its beauty to be so intimidating, so overpowering that I could never sit directly under it. I feared being consumed by it, though this sounds odd to admit. I only ever sat a dozen or so yards away, angled so that I could glimpse it only out of my peripheral vision. I felt so small and stunned whenever I let myself take all of it in. It was the same sort of feeling I get when I stop to think of how small I am relative to the vastness of the universe.

I thought about this willow tree often during my last term at Oxford as I was working on an independent study focused on religion, politics, and the environment under Andrew's supervision—the same tutor I had the previous term for mysticism and my unofficial therapist my first term at Oxford. Employing the term "eco-consciousness," I was exploring the different ways that individuals, religious and non-religious, visualize their relationship to the environment and engage with the reality of environmental degradation and climate change. In my conversations with Andrew, we came to an interesting distinction between relating to the environment on a global versus local scale.

Global eco-consciousness emphasizes the interconnectedness of ecosystems. It takes a big-picture view of how living things relate to and depend upon one another in the vast web of life we are all caught up in. Buddhism offers us a particularly powerful metaphor for visualizing our relationship to the environment in the metaphor of the deity Indra's net. In this metaphor, there is a net that hangs over Indra's palace, and at each intersection point, there is a multifaceted, glittering jewel.[33] Each jewel reflects all other jewels, no matter their distance. We might imagine that each jewel represents a living being, an atom, or a unit of consciousness. However defined, each jewel is connected to the others by the net and through their shared reflections.

Indra's net tells us that nothing that exists does so on its own. Each of us is bound to all things through complex ties. Each of us contains multitudes; we are all microcosms of the universe. I am but one jewel embedded in an infinite web, reflecting the grand weeping willow tree as it reflects my own image back at me.

Since we are all caught up in one big net, we should not only be concerned about the environmental well-being of our imminent surroundings, but also the well-being of the entire Earth. Because climate change knows no borders, our concern shouldn't either. I worry for Venice's rising waters, just as I worry about the devastating hurricanes in Puerto Rico and the Amazon aflame. This is no artificial concern. My very well-being is caught up with the well-being of the weeping willow, the hungry stray dog who lives on my street, the stranger

33   Jon Kabat-Zinn, "Indra's Net at Work: The Mainstreaming of Dharma Practice in Society," in *The Psychology of Awakening: Buddhism, Science, and Our Day-To-Day Lives*, ed. Gay Watson, Stephen Batchelor, and Guy Claxton (York Beach: Red Wheel/Weiser, 2000), pp. 225-249, 225.

sleeping on a park bench in the cold, the Amazon rain forest, and my mom who quieted her suffering with drugs. Picture suffering as a disruptive vibration. When there is suffering in the world, it echoes through the ties that connect us all. I do not escape unscathed from the burning of the Amazon, Mom's drug use and lack of access to resources that would have helped her, or a society that allows for fellow human beings to live on the streets in the cold.

In contrast with global eco-consciousness, local eco-consciousness emphasizes gaining familiarity and intimacy with one's surroundings as the first key step to conceptualizing and engaging with climate change. In *Staying Put: Making a Home in a Restless World*, Scott Sanders says, "If we are to reshape our way of thinking to fit the way of things ... many more of us need to know our local ground, walk over it, care for it, fight for it, bear it steadily in mind."[34]

If we are to adapt to the reality of climate change, we must shift the way we think about and relate to our surroundings. We must seek out a more intimate relationship with our environment. This intimacy may be built by learning more about our local grounds and their inhabitants, by walking through places we normally speed through, and by investing in the well-being of our local surroundings. In building intimacy, we might ask ourselves questions like: what makes this landscape unique compared with others I've visited? How has this landscape changed in recent decades? What are some small changes that need to happen in order to better care for it? And what are some larger ones?

---

34 Scott Russell Sanders, *Earth Works: Selected Essays* (Bloomington: Indiana University Press, 2012), 122.

Sanders' notion of coming to "know our local ground" is quite striking when I reflect back on how transient I have been for the majority of my life. This is not only my experience; in my circles of friends, it is a relatively rare occurrence to stay put in a place. Despite my constant wandering, I have often experienced this connection to place that Sanders speaks of. I suspect this is because I am an avid walker and enjoy taking the time to recognize the uniqueness of each place I encounter. There have been many places in my life in which I have lived and loved. I consider these places as friends. I took the time to learn about their existence before I arrived. I tell stories about them to friends and strangers as if the places themselves are someone they must meet. This is the way I feel about Port Meadow and the massive weeping willow tree. This is the way I feel about my family's home in the forested town of Magalia and our old home in the Mojave Desert.

To love a place is to be devoted to its well-being. Cities are not just storehouses of goods to consume but places deserving of our attention and care. Our rural lands are not warehouses of raw materials but places for other beings to live and an escape from the built-up and tightly packed environments of cities. How we treat the places we live and the Earth we call home may not impact all of our futures, but it will certainly have an impact on the futures of all of our descendants. As the Earth continues to warm, the oceans acidify, the ice caps melt, the forests burn, and deserts and diseases spread, few—if any—of us humans will be able to escape the fallout of our planetary home in distress.

I think most of us have experienced a deep attachment to a particular place or set of places. What places have you loved? Where do you call home? Building intimacy with our local environment serves as a good jumping-off point for visualizing the very personal threat of climate change. We can all imagine what the pain of losing a place we love deeply might feel like. Or at the very least, we can imagine that it would be very unpleasant, and if given the chance, we would do a lot to stop it from happening.

Of course, we can relate to the environment and the reality of climate change with both global and local perspectives. Global and local forms of eco-consciousness are simply different ways to think about our connectivity to place, environment, and each other as we face the ultimate existential threat that is climate change. The intimacy that comes with deep familiarity with a place is a concrete manifestation of the more abstract reality of our connectivity to and dependence upon all else that exists.

Developing our own eco-consciousness is a good first step toward internalizing what is at stake should harmful environmental practices continue. The greatest dangers to the environment's well-being are our proclivities for indifference, denial, and the paralysis of despair. If we do not care about climate change, refuse to acknowledge its existence, or do not compel ourselves to take action against it, we are condemning the Earth and its inhabitants. Of course, it is important to note that we do not all share equal blame. Just one hundred companies are responsible for 71 percent of greenhouse gas emissions. Individual actions and impacts are almost negligible when compared to such an outsized impact by these entities.[35]

35   Tess Riley, "Just 100 Companies Responsible for 71% of Global Emissions, Study Says," *The Guardian*, July 10, 2017.

All we can do is insist that those companies and their investors that are contributing the majority of emissions recognize our shared, hastened, existential vulnerability should we continue on the path that we are on. Recognition of this threat will require a widespread shift in individuals' self-understanding outside of systems that value only short-term profits and consumption. We cannot continue operating as a country, as nations, with only short-term profits in mind. Only when the large impact makers admit that there is something more significant than profits at stake do we have a chance at mitigating the massive impacts of climate change that are sure to come—and for some have already arrived.

We are not and cannot be stuck with the status quo—it is able to be otherwise. Together, we can breathe to life a world that is more gentle and more compassionate toward all living beings, where the value placed on the health and well-being of the planet and all of its sentient inhabitants cannot be summed up by price tags.

Paradise is an old California Gold Rush town that burst into existence when flocks of gold seekers arrived. A railroad map from 1900 suggests that the town used to be named Pair-O-Dice after a local saloon of the same name, however there are no corroborating documents or explanations.[36] Another legend says that the town got its name sometime in the 1860s when a guy by the name of William Leonard had returned to the area after a hard day's work in the valley.

Sitting in the shade of a towering pine tree, he is rumored to have sighed, saying to his crew: "Boys, this is paradise."[37]

---

36   David Mikkelson, "Place Name Origins: Paradise, California," Snopes, September 19, 2013.

37   Ibid.

Teressa's index finger bolts up above her head, interrupting my conversation with Jay. We are sitting in our California home in the hills above Redding, up near the Oregon border. "There's a fire at Canyon Road near China Gulch," she says. "Thought it'd be worth interrupting your conversation."

It's the summer of 2020, and in familiar fashion, my body starts to slump, a long sigh exhaled through my nose as I remind myself to remain calm, to breathe, to react rationally. Every fiber of my being wants to burst into tears, to lie on the floor, and to be consumed. The constant stress of having everything materially precious to me ripped from me in a California blaze is beyond exhausting. California summers now mean living in fear for my family, our cats, and our lives. Each time I hear a mention of yet another wildfire, I can't help but recall how I watched helpless as the Camp Fire razed Paradise to the ground in 2018.

My family moved to Magalia, a small and more densely forested town right above Paradise, when I was a sophomore in high school. It was there that I first discovered my love of walking. Though it took me just under two hours to get from Magalia to school each morning with the commute—a combination of walking and riding the regional bus line, as I passed through the town of Paradise and then into Chico—I loved living in the mountains amid the trees. I loved the way they smelled after a heavy rain and the snow they carried in the winter. I spent many of my days walking among them, sometimes alone and sometimes with friends who were kind enough to make the commute to visit me. I was drawn to the different sorts of moss that grew on the trees' bark, the mushrooms that grew on the carcasses of older felled trees, the crunch of pine needles, and crispy leaves underfoot.

I was interested in the miscellaneous discarded objects I came across on my hikes: the deflated basketballs, old Big Gulp cups from the 7-Eleven one town over, broken beer bottles, discarded assorted footwear, and empty candy wrappers. Sometimes I'd meet fellow neighbors on my walks who were either in search of an adventure like me or walking their dogs. I'd often talk with them awhile and hear their stories of why they had moved up into the mountains, how some things have changed, and how others have not at all.

Over the years, I grew familiar with the rhythms of these tree-canopied woods. Each season had its own sounds, its own music, that sounded when I traversed the landscape. In the dead of winter, the creek would be frozen, and sometimes I'd dare to step on it. In the summer, the creek cooled me down as I walked through it, eyes fixed to the creek bed looking for polished rocks to bring home and place on my family's porch. The polished rocks witnessed to me from my family's porch, reminding me of all that I had learned in the woods. Through my walks, I got to know the places that I'm from, the community that surrounds me, and myself just a bit more.

These memories of walks I cherish. I will never be able to replicate such walks again. The woods are different now.

The Camp Fire burned through these woods along with the towns of Paradise, Magalia, Concow, and Pulga in November 2018. Only about 5 percent of the buildings in Paradise survived without serious damage.[38] I had sat helpless for days on end as the story developed: the Camp Fire had burned at the pace of a football field each second, forty-four acres a minute.[39]

I had gone through the motions then. I continued to go to class, write my papers, and show up to work. I was paralyzed by the pictures and videos where the town appeared disfigured and aflame, so alien from the trees and the landscapes of my memories. I said I was "doing all right" when asked. When I would finally make it to my dorm room, my private sanctuary, I would burst into tears.

Pounding my bed with my fists, I sobbed until I was breathless, until my legs gave out beneath me and I sunk to the hard and unvacuumed floor. I experimented to see if screaming or throwing things would help. I lobbed my pillows at the opposite wall and screamed into my comforter, but nothing seemed to help relieve the searing pain of loss I felt inside. I repeated this ritual for days on end in the home I shared with Emily, Laura, and Daniel. I kept thinking about how I had imagined losing a place I loved on that plane back to Oxford less than a year ago. *I don't have to imagine anymore*, I thought wryly to myself.

Whenever my tears subsided and I was not in class, I couldn't stop checking the news or watching the videos that depicted a place I loved horribly transfixed and villainous as monstrous flames threatened the lives of

38   Mallory Moench, "'People Are Soul Tired:' 2 Years after the Camp Fire Destroyed Paradise, Only a Fraction of Homes Have Been Rebuilt," *San Francisco Chronicle*, November 8, 2020.

39   Judson Jones, "One of the California Wildfires Grew So Fast It Burned the Equivalent of a Football Field Every Second," *CNN*, November 10, 2018.

those I cared about. Every second dragged painfully by as I waited to hear from Mikala, my favorite bus companion; Beverly, my fellow guitarist and travel companion in Kenya; Teressa's brother, Byron, and his wife Shannon, who had been taking care of my beloved childhood cat Squeak for the past couple years; and Lindsey, who had traveled with Teressa and me in Italy. It was days before I knew that all of my friends and family had made it out safe, days before I found out just how many of my friends and their families had lost everything.

My heart continues to ache for each acre that was burnt in the Camp Fire. Since I've never owned a car, my default measurement of distance is how long it will take me to walk somewhere. I imagine it would take me quite a while to walk from one end of the burn area to the other. In my grieving, I often found myself wandering the streets of Providence, superimposing the streets of Paradise onto the blocks surrounding Brown's campus. I walked through Paradise in my imagination as I headed from one class to another, to dinner, and back to my room, fondly recalling my favorite hiking trails, parks, and shops. My steps were as heavy as my heart.

While I tried to imagine the loss of human and non-human life from the fire, I struggled to fully comprehend it at such a distance: eighty-five Paradise residents dead and more than 18,000 structures destroyed.[40] These numbers are too large, too unfathomable, and too unprecedented. All I could imagine was a charred Paradise, devoid of its usual dartings of deer, chattering of birds, and friendly community members entering

40 "Camp Fire," Cal Fire, November 8, 2018.

and exiting shops. Now, when I drive through Paradise with my family nearly two years after the fire, I see the charred marks the fire left in its wake all around. But I also see the frames of new houses being built, the lines outside of food trucks, and cars queued as they wait to get their coffee from the popular regional chain, Dutch Bros. Slowly maturely life is returning, as new plants grow and new homes pop up, but it is a slow and painful effort—just as it is with grieving.

The outpouring of love and support for those impacted by the fire was astounding in the year that followed. The communities that were displaced were met with the support of other communities, near and far. I met many people throughout the rest of my time at Brown who informed me that they or someone they knew had traveled across the country to pitch in, whether that meant rescuing animals, helping distribute resources to the survivors, or beginning the immense cleanup effort.

Donald Trump visited Paradise on the seventeenth of November 2018. Standing against a backdrop of homes leveled by the fire, he mistakenly referred to the town as "Pleasure," in what I found to be the most absurd Freudian slip, not altogether unexpected given the character of the orator.[41] Trump blamed the intensity of the fire on anything but climate change, stating, instead, that it was solely a product of poor upkeep and not enough raking. Laughter can be a nice break in dark times, so I assuredly have to thank him for the gut laughter that followed his remarks.

---

41 "'Pleasure, What a Name:' Trump Confused over Fire-Hit Town Paradise – Video," *The Guardian*, November 18, 2018.

Landscapes are storehouses of memories. The cumulative loss, both material and mental, from the Camp Fire was and remains collectively immeasurable. It is an existential tragedy. Despite this loss, I have built new memories in these charred places. I have walked around my old neighborhood, celebrated as friends rebuilt their homes or found new ones, and enjoyed countless BBQs in the forest I love so dearly.

The Camp Fire is an environmental tragedy. It is one of many unprecedented wildfires that are a result of human-caused climate change. The Camp Fire is also a political event. It prompted the opinions of climate change deniers and pro-rakers such as Trump. Yet it also spurred collective actions that are remarkable testaments to the power of community and the power of the people in the face of disaster.

I'd always known that I would have to grieve for the loss of my loved ones. I had hoped, however, that I would never have to grieve for the loss of a place I loved. It's grueling, just like any other form of grief, and it has forever transformed me. I am now more aware than ever of the threat of climate change and the devastation it will continue to inflict should human beings continue to pollute at current levels. My deep concern for climate change was born from my deep love for the small forest communities that I called home for many years. My commitment to discussing climate change is fueled by the resiliency of these now-altered places.

Nearly two years after the Camp Fire, any fire near us throws my family and me into a panic. The fire at Canyon Road that Teressa announced was extinguished quickly. Just a couple hundred feet across, it was crushed rapidly with fire retardant and water dropped from red-and-white firefighting planes that flew low over our house. I had watched the planes slide across the sky toward the smoke as I lay on my back in Teressa's striped hammock in our garden, stress-eating tomatoes.

The aftermath of the small fire, however, lasted hours. We each packed a go bag with our favorite belongings, medications, and a few outfit changes. Walking around my room, I tried to discern what I treasured most. The truth was, I loved all four hundred of my books and could never decide. I couldn't help but recall my younger self who, only a couple of weeks after moving to Tijuana, had to gather up all of my belongings to sell. I was terrified at the thought of losing everything again.

"I'll pick in the moment," I muttered to myself, hoping the moment never came. That night, Jay insisted on falling asleep while sitting upright on the couch closest to the front of our house and the large bay window. I roused him when I headed to the kitchen to get ice cream.

"You're making too much noise," he said. I explained my intentions and the need to rummage through the freezer.

"But I'm trying to hear the sirens," he informed me through his yawn.

"I looked at the news reports, and there's nothing active," I said, hoping to comfort him. Still, he remained at his station.

In August 2020, hundreds of fires burned simultaneously across California. In a period of ten hot and stormy August days, Cal Fire reported that roughly

1.1 million acres had been burned.[42] For comparison, Rhode Island sits on 777,000 acres of land. California blazes had consumed an area larger than the state I had called home for the last five years in just over a week. By the end of the summer, blazes had consumed more than five Rhode Islands, setting a new modern record for California.[43] How do you even fathom a loss so substantial? So many acres of wonders marred by flame, so many animal and plant lives obliterated.

This sort of devastation is no longer unprecedented but expected.

For weeks, I stepped outside each morning to watch the sun struggle through the cloud of smoke that hung permanently suspended over Northern California: the sun an angry, hazy red. Ash rained from the sky, blanketing our garden in a light film composed of the remnants of burned trees and homes. I inhaled bits of ash as I worked in the garden, my asthma unable to handle being outdoors for more than twenty minutes at a time.

"West Coast cities have the worst air quality in the world," I read in several headlines covering the devastation of the summer 2020 wildfires.[44]

42   Tom Di Liberto, "Over a Million Acres Burned in California in Second Half of August 2020," Climate.gov, August 26, 2020.

43   Alex Wigglesworth and Joseph Serna, "California Fire Season Shatters Record with More Than 4 Million Acres Burned," *LA Times*, October 4, 2020.

44   Vivian Ho, "West Coast Cities Face the World's Worst Air Quality as Wildfires Rage," *The Guardian*, September 14, 2020.

In the wake of the Camp Fire, I found myself thinking a lot about grief, about Mom, and about love—of places and of people.

In loving someone, we are both powerful and powerless. In *Love's Work*, Gillian Rose, a former professor of social and political thought at Warwick University, writes about the demands of love, philosophy, and faith in the wake of her cancer diagnosis.[45] Considering the dynamics of love, Rose comes to the conclusion that an individual in a loving relationship is simultaneously in a position of complete power as well as a state of absolute vulnerability.[46] Either person in a love relationship has the power to break the other's heart and therefore bears the risk of having their heart broken.[47] It is this tension between power and powerlessness that constitutes the risky nature of love. To be in love is to assume constant risk and to accept one's limits that lay between power and powerlessness.

For Rose, this uncertainness, this vulnerability, is absolutely essential in a love relationship. It is the foundation of trust. Terry Tempest Williams also reflects on the risky business of love in her essay "Winter Solstice at the Moab Slough." She writes, "I think of my own stream of desires, how cautious I have become with love. It is a vulnerable enterprise to feel deeply and I may not survive my affections."[48]

I may not survive my affections.

---

45   Gillian Rose, *Love's Work* (London: Vintage, 1997).

46   Ibid, 68-69.

47   Ibid, 88-89.

48   Terry Tempest Williams, *An Unspoken Hunger* (New York: Knopf Doubleday Publishing Group, 2015).

There were many times after losing Mom that I thought I might not survive. I had taken the risk of loving her after years and years of her silence, and in the end, I was utterly and devastatingly heartbroken. The hardest part of losing someone you love is holding onto and preserving the memories of moments shared with them. Time, of course, ages all. Each time we summon a memory, we are gently transforming it, at times even rewriting it. The wounds from unweaving my life from hers have healed, yet I now feel as if I dreamed the whole thing. I no longer recognize her voice; I struggle to recall her face without looking at a photograph. It is no easy task to preserve good memories alongside the bad, but it is crucial that we do so. This book is, in many ways, an exercise in preserving the good alongside the bad.

Grieving for the loss of a loved one is different than grieving for the loss of a place. Though different, my grieving processes bled into one another. While many of my peers were trying to decide what they wanted to do after they graduated from Brown, I could hardly see further than a day ahead of me. I found it hard to talk in class or with friends and family. It wasn't until a friend cracked a joke one night and I laughed that I knew I was going to resurface from my grieving.

I am convinced that laughter has healing powers. In *Living a Feminist Life*, Sara Ahmed writes about laughter as a survival tool to be employed in the quest to dismantle the patriarchy. Ahmed writes ". . . Laughter can lighten our loads. In fact we laugh often in recognition of the shared absurdity of this world; or just in recognition of this world."[49]

---

49   Sara Ahmed, *Living a Feminist Life* (Durham: Duke University Press, 2017).

Each time I laughed with my friends after the fire or as I processed losing Mom while at Oxford, I felt myself becoming a bit lighter, a bit less weighed down by my grief. While laughter was by no means an absolute cure, it at least helped me return to the realm of the living and talking. Laughter helped me get a grip on what was holding me down and hold it at arm's length.

Laughter also became a vital activity that I shared with friends who were impacted by the Camp Fire as the lightening of our mental burdens became a group exercise in survival. As fires burned all around me in the summer of 2020, I laughed with friends as we marveled at those who still did not accept the reality of climate change. In sharing laughs, we were able to let out our pent-up bewilderment and anger. In this way, laughter is a tool for long-term social and political engagement. It is a vital re-energizer.

Once I was able to laugh again after the Camp Fire, I started going to a therapist for the first time in my life. My therapist told me something that I'll never forget.

"Do not think like a statistic," she told me.

"What do you mean?" I probed.

"Do not think like a statistic. I mean do not think something is going to happen to you just because it happens to others who are like you. You are more than a statistic."

Once I had wrapped my head around what she meant, I could feel the power of her statement and how radically transformative it was for me.

When I first came to my therapist broken by grief, I was equally worried about my shattered personal life as I was about the impact it was going to have on my performance at Brown. I had all of these statistics floating around my head which made me feel like I was always in danger of failing and slipping behind my peers. I knew that, for example, there were fewer first-generation students and peers in my income bracket at Brown than there were members of the top 0.1 percent.[50] I knew that 90 percent of first-generation, low-income students do not graduate with a bachelor's degree within six years of beginning university.[51] I knew many of my peers had had fancy unpaid internships that they had been able to accept, while I lacked comparable work experience, and so on.

While these statistics had served me in the past in terms of grounding myself in the context and barriers I was working with, I had come to internalize them in a more harmful way. I had all but convinced myself that I was destined to fail if I slipped even a little bit. Though I undid some of my harmful notions about productivity while I was at Oxford, I still felt like I had been somehow defying gravity for years and I was going to come crashing down if I took my eyes off the prize for too long.

All of this, coupled with my tendency to judge my worth based on my academic attainment, created a system that barely permitted me to grieve. I was horrified by the system but felt incapable of escaping it; I was scared to loosen my focus on my studies for fear of having to confront the tidal wave of grief that threatened to drown me.

---

50 "Economic Diversity and Student Outcomes at Brown University," *The Upshot, New York Times*, 2017.

51 "90% of Low-Income, First-Generation College Students Don't Graduate on Time," EAB, April 29, 2019.

Do not think like a statistic. This command echoed in my mind for weeks after my therapist first uttered it. While the transition to not thinking like a statistic was incredibly difficult, it was even more freeing. I had to internalize that I was worth more than my productivity, more than how my professors and peers received my work. I also had to re-convince myself that nothing bad was going to happen if I took a couple of days off. I didn't need to desperately grind away at work every day to be a good student and produce thoughtful products. Instead, I turned my attention to my friends and family. I took long walks for the sake of taking long walks, and I let myself mourn without trying to multitask and do my course readings at the same time.

There are structural barriers which inhibit us, and there are the ways in which we inhibit ourselves. The reality of structural barriers to attainment is unquestionable. But I think it is important to keep pushing and testing the resolve of such barriers. While a path blockaded with barriers is more tedious than a cleared path, you may be able to bring your own ladder along and slowly and maturely meander down your path. You'll undoubtedly need to rest along the way, as overcoming barriers gets tiresome, but it's possible. In journeying over the barriers I faced as a first-generation and low-income student, I like to imagine that I and students like me are slowly wearing the barriers down, making them a bit more surmountable for others who come after us. Hopefully, our efforts will prove that things are able to be otherwise, despite the ways they seem determined to be.

I graduated on a hot day in June surrounded by my favorite people. Jay, Teressa, Justin, Lisa, and Allegra all flew to Providence to celebrate. I took them on tours around my favorite Providence sights: the woodblock prints at the Rhode Island School of Design's museum, the waterside path along the downtown canal, and my favorite local coffee shops.

My graduation ceremony began with a procession through the center of Brown's campus, through the Van Wickle Gates and down several Brown-alumni-lined streets to reach the oldest Baptist church in the United States. Surrounded by my friends, I felt an overwhelming sense of pride and gratitude for our time together. My sadness at the end of our journey served as a testament to the strong bonds we had built with one another.

As we passed through the Van Wickle gates to confront what seemed like thousands of Brown alumni lined up and down the streets cheering for us, I made eye contact with alum John Krasinski.

"Laura!" I shouted, tapping her on the shoulder, "It's John. Do you want a picture?"

Before I could finish my question, Laura was pulling the rest of our group toward John. Surrounding him on all sides, our group semi-successfully shoved ourselves into the camera's frame and snapped a selfie, one highlight of my day only to be beaten by the feeling that came hours later when my diploma was placed in my hands.

Only after I received my diploma and sat back down in the small room that consisted of graduating seniors who had concentrated in religious studies and their families did I realize what my brother had written on the chalkboard behind the speakers.

$A^2 + B^2 = C^2$, or Anna + Brown = Change the World.

I leaned forward to stare over at my brother in horror and then with gratitude. This was his way of expressing he was proud of me. It has since become a favorite mantra among some of my friends who like to see my cheeks flush red.

I passed my diploma down the row of loved ones there to support me. It was as much theirs as it was mine. Without their love and support, I knew I wouldn't be holding the Latin-inscribed document in my hands that represented over $300,000 of Grey Goose Vodka money that had been invested in me.

I had applied to stay at Brown for a one-year master's in public affairs at the start of May just four weeks before I graduated. I hadn't made it through the early round interview of a dream job to study experiences of poverty throughout the United States. While I had the qualitative expertise to capture individuals' narratives, I did not have the quantitative or technical expertise to analyze the impacts of certain government programs and life experiences on those living in poverty. The brochure for the master's program at Brown was almost word for word what my dream job had told me I was lacking.

Two weeks before my graduation, I heard back from the program. I had been accepted with full funding; the director of the program informed me in her office as I stared back at her in shock, mouth agape.

"Thank you. Thank you so much." I reminded myself to breathe. *Inhale. Exhale.* "This means so much to me. I can't thank you enough."

"We're happy to have you in the program," the director said, smiling. "Your recommenders spoke highly of you, and we know you'll bring your passion for helping others to the program."

"I promise I will." I walked the two blocks back to my dorm room alternating between laughing and crying. The funding had been completely unexpected, and the relief of knowing what I was going to do next with my life was liberating.

I started the program one week after I graduated and took out enough loans to pay for a year's worth of rent for a bedroom in an aged, three-story Victorian home just a handful of blocks from campus. The day I moved in, a couple of the bathroom ceiling tiles collapsed in mushy shards on the bathroom floor after absorbing water from a leaking toilet on the floor above. This pretty much set the tone for life in this well-worn home.

I began graduate school with intensive summer courses in statistics and economics, and I soon discovered that I had a lot to learn. Many of my classmates were older than me, and some had quite a lot of career experience. I was one of the few who had no previous background in public policy, statistics, or economics. To say the least, I was far outside of my comfort zone, much further than I'd ever been before. But I knew that I had been invested in for a reason.

Just as I did in undergrad, I committed to working hard since I was fortunate enough to have the financial support of others. I wanted to learn how to best do good for others in recognition of the money and opportunities that allowed me to do good for myself. But the more I learned about the issues—how to quantify them and different ways of addressing them—the humbler I became. It's easy to say something has to be fixed, but it's very difficult to put a fix into practice. Even when a fix is implemented, there are all sorts of unintended consequences that come about. This element of risk is unavoidable when we are working with complex issues and incomplete knowledge.

When I wasn't learning about policy, I was spending time with Jackie and David. David, one of my dear friends from my undergraduate years at Brown who had lived on my same floor freshman year, remained at Brown to pursue medicine. His presence made Providence feel like home, even though everyone else we knew had moved away.

I had met Jackie on my second day of orientation. From the first day we met, there were not many days that I spent at Brown without Jackie by my side. With an endless supply of good memes, Jackie was always ready to make me laugh. An extremely hard worker, Jackie does everything that she does to the best of her ability and often in the service of others. My role model and my rock throughout graduate school, Jackie was someone I could vent to that as a fellow first-generation and low-income student would understand the difficulties I was navigating.

Jackie, David, and I had dinner together at least twice a week. We'd often cook in my house, as my roommates were seldom there throughout the entire year. On weekends, we'd often all hole up in my room and work on our laptops, drinking coffee and munching on donuts to tide us over until dinner. It was my first time living alone outside of the dorms, and their company meant the world to me. Ten-hour study-and-work days became tolerable when I had dinner with them to look forward to. The decaying Victorian home I lived in became livable when we could laugh about its poor condition together. When laughing it off didn't work, I reminded myself that it was not the worst place I had ever lived, thinking back to low-budget Tijuana motels and nights spent roaming the streets.

In my first few months of policy school, the magnitude and severity of issues like poverty, addiction, and climate change became clearer to me. With greater clarity, however, came a growing sense of despair. I was frustrated about how slow things seemed to change in these policy areas. I was also frustrated by the fact that there were still so many discussions surrounding if anything should even be done.

Inaction in these areas is, in part, a product of stigma—what we may think of as a set of negative assumptions or judgments that certain people experience from others that result in them being discriminated against, rejected, and/or excluded from certain areas of society.[52] Stigma manifests in statements like, "Poor people are poor because they are lazy," or because they "don't have the right mind-set" or "Individuals experiencing addiction don't deserve compassion or help because they are electing to get high and they bear the blame." We might even think of those who accept the reality of climate change as bearing a certain stigma. They may be framed as threatening the stability of short-term profits and jobs, while having "no real grounds" for their beliefs.

The most impactful part of my master's program ended up being a three-month consultancy where I got to learn about addiction and work on community-based programs to combat the stigma surrounding addiction. I spent three months working at the Clinton Foundation's New York City branch, housed in a skyscraper just a handful of blocks away from Times Square. Emily, my travel companion and friend from Brown, and her family were kind enough to offer me housing on the third floor of their home in Brooklyn. So I found myself commuting from Brooklyn to Manhattan every weekday, dressed in business casual clothing and pressed up against other

52   *The World Health Report 2001: Mental Health: New Understanding, New Hope* (World Health Organization, 2001), 16.

commuters clutching newspapers, smartphones, and coffees in crowded subway cars.

The irony of working at the Clinton Foundation was not lost on me. Just two years ago, I had been sitting at Oxford, marveling that everyone at the table had some connection to the Clintons. Just two years ago, I had sat in the Oxford Union—a university forum for high-profile speakers and debates—and listened to Monica Lewinsky talk about her life after Bill Clinton. Constantly bombarded by death threats and negative portrayals in the media, she had been forced into seclusion for a number of years to eventually emerge as a strong anti-bullying advocate.[53] I knew she never would have faced such strong backlash and public shaming if she weren't a woman. I cried listening to her story, marveling at how she was not only able to rebuild her life but use her experiences to help others. Then here I was, watching Bill Clinton get ushered in and out of the building by a cadre of well-dressed secret service agents.

Though conflicted about taking a position at the Clinton Foundation, I was thankful for the opportunity to learn more about addiction and the Foundation's effort to decrease stigma in faith communities across the United States. I believed that the Foundation's strategy of educating faith leaders around the nation on addiction and equipping them to reduce the stigma surrounding addiction in their communities was not only a unique approach, but a damn smart one.[54]

---

53 Monica Lewinsky, "Shame and Survival," *Vanity Fair*, June 2014.

54 "Engaging Community Leaders," Clinton Foundation, accessed March 1, 2021.

Faith leaders, I knew, had unique power and influence in their communities, and I was excited to see a real-world example of people of different faiths coming together to address an issue as daunting as addiction. If faith leaders could come together to address addiction and help those who were struggling, they could do the same for climate change and poverty.

While at the Foundation, I read up on all the ways addiction had been mismanaged historically and presently, in large part because of stigma. Addiction had long been viewed—and still is viewed—by many as a moral failing, not a chronic disease in need of treatment. Stigma surrounding substance use disorders (synonymous with "addiction") blames the individual using a substance for any poor health outcomes resulting from their use. The 1999 U.S. Surgeon General's Report on Mental Health described the impact of stigma as eroding confidence that a particular condition is a valid and treatable health condition.[55] Thinking of this in light of the opioid crisis, we can say that the stigma surrounding addiction isolates those struggling with addiction and makes treatment and recovery pathways and resources less accessible.

As the opioid epidemic continues to evolve and claim the lives of tens of thousands of Americans, there are countless individuals struggling with addiction who do not have the care, support, or resources they need. My mom was one of many who never received the care and support she needed. I needed to know why Mom never got help. Was it because she did not want help? Or was it because

---

55 *Dispelling the Myths and Stigma of Mental Illness: The Surgeon General's Report on Mental Health* (National Health Policy Forum, April 14, 2000).

she was too self-conscious to come out and ask for help at the risk of experiencing intense judgment? Was it because we did not have the money to afford a resource as scarce as treatment? Or did she never ask for help because her substance use was tied up with mental health conditions that she also never received treatment for?

Stigma is embedded within the American health care system itself. There is a disparity of funding for research and treatment of mental health and substance use disorders as compared with physical disorders in the US health care system.[56] This disparity translates into limited access to the behavioral health treatment and other services that those struggling with addiction would benefit from.[57]

Over 7 percent of the United States population struggles with addiction, yet not everyone who struggles with addiction can access treatment.[58] In 2019, over 20 percent of individuals who deemed substance use treatment as necessary did not receive it due to their inability to afford the treatment and the fact that it was not covered by their insurance.[59] Over 20 percent of individuals reported not receiving treatment because they didn't know where to go. If we don't make it easy for people to locate resources,

---

56 Committee on the Science of Changing Behavioral Health Social Norms, *Ending Discrimination against People with Mental and Substance Use Disorders: The Evidence for Stigma Change* (Washington: National Academy of Sciences, 2016), 45-46.

57 Ibid.

58 *Key Substance Use and Mental Health Indicators in the United States: Results from the 2019 National Survey on Drug Use and Health* (Rockville: Substance Abuse and Mental Health Services Administration, 2020), 41.

59 Ibid, B-20.

many will err away from asking, for fear of discrimination and judgment. Moreover, nearly 17 percent of individuals did not pursue treatment due to potential negative economic impacts on their current employment, compounding the financial inaccessibility of treatment and the stigma attached to using such resources.[60]

Finally, 17 percent of individuals who felt that they needed treatment within the last twelve months did not receive it because they thought such treatment would negatively impact their neighbors' or community's opinion of them.[61] These individuals erred away from receiving treatment for fear of how those around them would react.

In these statistics, we glimpse the reality that a large share of individuals struggling with addiction do not receive help because of the stigma that is embedded within the American health care system and the stigma that is embedded within their very communities, families, and workplaces. Those who condemn and dismiss those battling addiction are inhibiting them from getting the treatment they need. How we talk about issues and the people who experience them matter, and in the case of addiction, the very way we talk about the issue impacts its magnitude.

As I pored through public health studies and reports at the Foundation, Mom remained at the forefront of my mind. I was learning about how strongly her health had been influenced by her environment, opportunities, and resources. I learned that there was significant overlap between mental illness and addiction. I knew she had lacked much of the early help she needed to address

---

60 Ibid.

61 Ibid.

her mental health issues and, later on, the resources she needed to treat her substance use issues. There were many times I forced myself to choke back tears as I sat at my desk. My whole framework for thinking about addiction was being rewritten, and in dangerous moments, I let myself wonder about how things might have been different if Mom had received the treatment she needed for her addiction and mental health issues.

I now dream of a day when addiction is universally understood as a chronic, neurological disorder requiring medical attention and is treated as seriously as other chronic conditions, such as cancer and diabetes.[62] I believe that my dream is possible, that the way we as a society talk about and treat addiction is able to be otherwise. It starts with individuals and their communities, which is why I was so excited to work with the Foundation's program to train and equip faith leaders with the tools to address addiction in their communities. By the end of the program, faith leaders were ready to educate others in their community with authority as they drew on concepts of love, acceptance, and healing from their respective traditions.

Sitting in a room filled with Atlanta-based faith leaders in February 2020, I recalled the many times that Mom had turned to the Christian Church for guidance and comfort during my childhood. I imagined what it would have been like if the Pentecostal pastor who often prayed over her would have also been equipped with the knowledge and language to guide her toward mental health and addiction resources in our community.

---

62   *Facing Addiction in America: The Surgeon General's Report on Alcohol, Drugs, and Health* (Washington: US Department of Health and Human Services, 2016), v.

Epilogue

When COVID first began taking over the world in March 2020, I headed home to Jay and Teressa's house in the hills of Northern California to finish up my graduate degree. No longer able to venture out into the world, I began dreaming of the world I wanted to emerge once the pandemic subsided.

It looks a little bit like this . . .

I dream of a world where we do not blame people who are trying to mute their suffering with substances but lend them our empathy and care. I dream of a world where even if our homes are currently safe from the effects of climate change, we care that others' homes are aflame, flooded, or frozen. I dream of a world where poverty is understood not as an individual failing or as a product of laziness but as a system failure, symptomatic of the way our society and economic systems devalue certain people and certain jobs.

It is through our breaths that demand change and the leaps of faith we take in believing that change is possible that we will breathe a future into existence that values all of our breaths. It will take many breaths and many leapers, but there are a lot of us.

And while I dream of this world to be breathed into existence, I think of Mom.

My dream is simply of a world that would allow me to take a walk with Mom in the heat of California summer without breathing in smoke. It is a world where though she suffered from depression and abuse, Mom would have been able to access the mental health care and substance treatment she needed. In this world to come, Mom's job as a secretary would have paid enough for us not to have had to live paycheck to paycheck, reliant on the kindness of strangers for our groceries.

There's not a day that passes when I don't think of Mom or wish that things would have ended differently between us. Amid the pain of our separation, I like to think of all of the ways that I am like my mom. I love to read and spell. I love to have adventures and travel. I am always looking for "aha" moments when life suddenly makes sense. Just as Mom decided to pack up our lives in Southern California and head to Tijuana when I was seven years old, I packed up my life in Northern California with Jay and Teressa in November 2020 and headed south for the border once again.

Staying in Oaxaca, then Chiapas, in southern Mexico, I have been revisiting the foods and language of my youth. It is my first time back in Mexico for any significant amount of time in thirteen years. Since I have been back, I have felt closer to Mom again. If I cannot be with her, at least I can live in the country she chose to call home. If I cannot see her again, at least I can spend my time helping create the sort of world where our lives together would have been otherwise: a world where Mom and I were together, healthy, and safe.

As I eat french fries with ketchup from street vendors, I am brought back to the Tijuana hotel where Mom and I narrowly beat pneumonia and feasted from the french fry cart outside. When I walk the streets at night in the brisk air, I imagine Mom is walking along beside me, keeping me company. I try to imagine what our walks would have been like together years and years ago if we were not concerned about making enough money for food and her supply. On Christmas, I ate tamales, just like Mom and I used to do with Alex and his family. On New Year's, I stood on a roof in Oaxaca and admired the fireworks that neighbors set off from their enclosed yards, cheering for my favorites just as I had done side by side with Mom.

Every day, I long to tell Mom that I am sorry for leaving her behind and that I love her. I wish she would have let me comfort her at her bedside when she was sick and let me tell her about my life and who I had become. I wish I could have eased more of her suffering to make life's burden a bit less heavy for her. I wish I truly knew her: the sound of her voice and the lines of her face. I'll never be able to do or know these things; and that's all right.

I do not think life is about closure.

I record these longings of the heart merely so they can be witnessed: if not by Mom, then at least by others. I share my life's most intimate moments because there is comfort in community and in finding others who struggle in ways familiar to one's own.

After meticulously compiling these records of my breaths, I now find that I am able to breathe easier. I am lighter, less tethered to the past. I have excavated all of my bad memories and memorialized them alongside the good. They are all a part of me that I accept—as integral to who I am as the breath that flows in and out of my lungs. I hope that by sharing these records of my breaths, we move just a little bit closer to a world where everyone can breathe easier.

Acknowledgements

For someone who is incredibly intimidated by large undertakings, I recognize that this book would not have been possible without the love and support of many.

Special thanks to Eric Koester and the New Degree Press team for making this all possible, my beta readers who helped me bring my book to its final form, and to my editors Kathy Wood and Alexander Pyles for your guidance and expertise.

Thank you to my high school teachers, college professors, and mentors for nurturing my love for learning. Marysol De La Torre-Escobedo, Rebekah Brown, Katie Raymond, Linnea Smith, Deborah Travers, Carrie Nordlund, Daniel Vaca, Neil Thakral, Jeffrey Moser, J. Nicholas Ziegler, Andrew Teal, Alexis Glenn, and Daniel Santos—I have learned so much from all of you that I carry with me each and every day.

I am grateful for my friends who believed I could write a book before I believed it myself. To my high school friends—Haylee Newman, Allegra Taylor, Mikala Butson, Beverly Vincent, Liv Leach, Angela Powers, and Jude Hand—thank you for the many years of love and laughs. To my college friends—Emily Henning, Laura

Bosque, Marianna McMurdock, Cole Adams, Samantha Cardet, David Wiegn, Jacqueline Agustin, Edward Brooke, Miriam Himelstein, Scooty Nickerson, Asey Koh, Eric Smith, and Ayesha Harisinghani—it'll be hard to look back and say my college years weren't the best of my life because y'all are incredible.

To everyone who preordered a copy of my book, I owe you my deepest thanks. My book is now published thanks to your early interest and generosity. Thank you to all of the aforementioned individuals and Adam Brock, Alex Dahl, Alexandra Ayoob, Aliosha Bielenberg, Amy Quinto, Ariana Zukergood, Bianca Leggett, Catharine Smith, Celeste Cramer, Chandran Sankaran, Chrissy Holm, Christina Tolomeo, Christopher Calley, Constance Gamache, Cynthia Guy, Dan Fitzgerald, Dan La Bar, Dena Newman, Eesha Bhave, Emily Sauter, Jameson Boyd, Jarrah Myles, Jennifer Bush, Jennifer DeSanctis, John Marcom, John Vincent, Keely Johnson, Kiera Johnson, Laila Tarraf, Leticia Calvillo, Lexie Ross, Lisa Higbee, Manuel Ávalos, Marjorie Henning, Mason Wong, Michael Butson, Miranda Martone, Misbah Noorani, Nanelle Taylor, Natalie Pilla, Patty Haley, Raj Salhotra, Robyn Sundlee, Ryan Bentley, Sacha de Jong, Sophia Davidson, Sophie Sandoe, Thanh-Thao Do, Tiffany Kuban, Willow Higgins, and Yunni Cho.

And last but not least, thank you to my family. To Jay and Teressa—words cannot express my gratitude for all that you've done for me. I hope this book serves as a start. To Justin and Lisa—thank you for filling my days with fun and excitement and for loving me unconditionally. To my Aunt Sue—thank you for always cheering me on. And to Squeak—there's no one I'd rather spend a night on the couch watching TV with than you.

Appendix

––––

Introduction

Lakner, Christoph, Nishant Lonzan, Daniel Mahler, R. Andres Castaneda Aguilar, and Haoyu Wu. "Updated Estimates of the Impact of COVID-19 on Global Poverty: Looking Back at 2020 and the Outlook for 2021." *World Bank Blogs*, January 11, 2021. https://blogs.worldbank.org/opendata/updated-estimates-impact-covid-19-global-poverty-looking-back-2020-and-outlook-2021#:~:text=The%20estimated%20increase%20in%20global%20poverty%20in%202020%20is%20truly%20unprecedented.&text=For%20the%20first%20time%20in,(downside%20estimate)%20in%202020.

Chapter One

Dixon, Amanda. "A Growing Percentage of Americans Have No Emergency Savings Whatsoever." Bankrate. July 1, 2019. https://www.bankrate.com/banking/savings/financial-security-june-2019/.

"Key Statistics & Graphics." United States Department of Agriculture Economic Research Service, September 9, 2020. https://www.ers.usda.gov/topics/food-nutrition-assistance/food-security-in-the-us/key-statistics-graphics.

aspx#:~:text=Among%20U.S.%20households%20with%20
children,households%20with%20children%20in%20
2019.&text=Both%20children%20and%20adults%20
were,children%20(2.4%20million%20households).

"SNAP-Eligible Households." Feeding America. Accessed
February 28, 2021. https://hungerandhealth.feedingamerica.
org/explore-our-work/programs-target-populations/
snap-eligible-households/#:~:text=The%20nutrition%20
assistance%20program%20reaches,42%20million%20
people%20each%20year.

"Study: 53% of US Adults Don't Have Emergency Fund." First
National Bank of Omaha, press release, February 19, 2020.
FNBO website. https://www.fnbo.com/insights/2020/
newsroom/fnbo-releases-2020-financial-planning-survey/
index.html.

Chapter Two

Centers for Disease Control and Prevention. "Understanding
the Epidemic." Updated March 19, 2020. https://www.cdc.
gov/drugoverdose/epidemic/index.html.

Guy, Gery P., Kun Zhang, Michele K. Bohm, Jan Losby, Brian
Lewis, Randall Young, Louise B. Murphy, Deborah Dowell.
"Vital Signs: Changes in Opioid Prescribing in the United
States, 2006-2015." *Morbidity and Mortality Weekly Report*
66, no. 26 (July 7, 2017): 697–704. https://www.cdc.gov/
mmwr/volumes/66/wr/mm6626a4.htm.

Phillips, Jonathan K., Morgan A. Ford, and Richard J. Bonnie,
eds. "Pain Management and the Opioid Epidemic: Balancing
Societal and Individual Benefits and Risks of Prescription
Opioid Use." *PubMed*. National Academies Press, (July 13,
2017). https://pubmed.ncbi.nlm.nih.gov/29023083/.

Chapter Eight

Alexander, Michelle. *The New Jim Crow: Mass Incarceration in the Age of Colorblindness*. New York: New Press, 2012.

Appelbaum, Binyamin. "Out of Trouble, but Criminal Records Keep Men Out of Work." *New York Times*, February 28, 2015. https://www.nytimes.com/2015/03/01/business/out-of-trouble-but-criminal-records-keep-men-out-of-work.html.

NAACP. "Criminal Justice Fact Sheet." Accessed February 28, 2021. https://www.naacp.org/criminal-justice-fact-sheet/.

Nishimura, Eshin, and Giei Satō. *Unsui: A Diary of Zen Monastic Life*. Honolulu: University of Hawaii Press, 1983.

Chapter Nine

Hannay, Alastair. *Kierkegaard: A Biography*. Cambridge: Cambridge University Press, 2001.

Kierkegaard, Søren. *Fear and Trembling*. A&D Books, 2014.

Thoreau, Henry David. *Walden and Civil Disobedience*. Digireads. com, 2013.

Chapter Ten

Atlas Obscura. "Budapest Cave Church." Accessed March 1, 2021. https://www.atlasobscura.com/places/budapest-cave-church.

Red Light District Tours. "10 Amsterdam Red Light District Safety Measures." November 7, 2017. https://www.amsterdamredlightdistricttour.com/news/10-safety-measures-for-prostitutes-in-the-red-light-district/.

Chapter Eleven

Berry, Nikki. "Venice Floods: Climate Change behind Highest Tide in 50 Years, Says Mayor." *BBC*, November 13, 2019. https://www.bbc.com/news/world-europe-50401308#:~:text=Severe%20flooding%20in%20Venice%20that,must%20listen%2C%22%20he%20added.

Dillard, Annie. *Pilgrim at Tinker Creek*. London: HarperCollins Publishers Ltd., 2007.

Kabat-Zinn, Jon. "Indra's Net at Work: The Mainstreaming of Dharma Practice in Society." In *The Psychology of Awakening: Buddhism, Science, and Our Day-To-Day Lives*, edited by Gay Watson, Stephen Batchelor, and Guy Claxton, 225–49. York Beach: Red Wheel/Weiser, 2000.

Laing, Olivia. *The Lonely City*. Edinburgh: Canongate Books Ltd., 2016.

Riley, Tess. "Just 100 Companies Responsible for 71% of Global Emissions, Study Says." The Guardian, July 10, 2017. https://www.theguardian.com/sustainable-business/2017/jul/10/100-fossil-fuel-companies-investors-responsible-71-global-emissions-cdp-study-climate-change.

Sanders, Scott Russell. *Earth Works: Selected Essays*. Bloomington: Indiana University Press, 2012.

"Sistine Chapel." Musei Vaticani. Accessed March 1, 2021. https://m.museivaticani.va/content/museivaticani-mobile/en/collezioni/musei/cappella-sistina/storia-cappella-sistina.html.

Chapter Twelve

Ahmed, Sara. *Living a Feminist Life*. Durham: Duke University Press, 2017.

Cal Fire. "Camp Fire." November 8, 2018. https://www.fire. ca.gov/incidents/2018/11/8/camp-fire/.

Di Liberto, Tom. "Over a Million Acres Burned in California in Second Half of August 2020." Climate.gov, August 26, 2020. https://www.climate.gov/news-features/event-tracker/over-million-acres-burned-california-second-half-august-2020.

EAB. "90% of Low-Income, First-Generation College Students Don't Graduate on Time." April 29, 2019. https://eab.com/insights/daily-briefing/student-success/90-of-low-income-first-generation-college-students-dont-graduate-on-time/.

"Economic Diversity and Student Outcomes at Brown University." *The Upshot, New York Times*, 2017. https://www.nytimes.com/interactive/projects/college-mobility/brown-university#:~:text=Brown%20University&text=The%20median%20family%20income%20of,but%20became%20a%20rich%20adult.&text=Below%2C%20estimates%2-0of%20how%20Brown,economic%20diversity%20and%20student%20outcomes.

Ho, Vivian. "West Coast Cities Face the World's Worst Air Quality as Wildfires Rage." *The Guardian*, September 14, 2020. https://www.theguardian.com/world/2020/sep/14/west-coast-air-quality-wildfires-oregon-california-washington.

Jones, Judson. "One of the California Wildfires Grew So Fast It Burned the Equivalent of a Football Field Every Second." *CNN*, November 10, 2018. https://www.cnn.com/2018/11/09/us/california-wildfires-superlatives-wcx.

Moench, Mallory. "'People Are Soul Tired:' 2 Years after the Camp Fire Destroyed Paradise, Only a Fraction of Homes Have Been Rebuilt." *San Francisco Chronicle*, November 8, 2020. https://www.sfchronicle.com/california-wildfires/article/People-are-soul-tired-2-years-after-the-15708762.php#:~:text=8%2C%202018%2C%20the%20blaze%20burned,of%20Paradise%20in%20November%202018.

"'Pleasure, What a Name:' Trump Confused over Fire-Hit Town Paradise – Video." *The Guardian*, November 18, 2018. https://www.theguardian.com/us-news/video/2018/nov/19/pleasure-what-a-name-trump-confused-over-fire-hit-town-paradise-video.

Rose, Gillian. *Love's Work*. London: Vintage, 1997.

Wigglesworth, Alex, and Joseph Serna. "California Fire Season Shatters Record with More Than 4 Million Acres Burned." *LA Times*, October 4, 2020. https://www.latimes.com/california/story/2020-10-04/california-fire-season-record-4-million-acres-burned.

Williams, Terry Tempest. *An Unspoken Hunger*. New York: Knopf Doubleday Publishing Group, 2015.

Chapter Thirteen

Committee on the Science of Changing Behavioral Health Social Norms. *Ending Discrimination against People with Mental and Substance Use Disorders: The Evidence for Stigma Change*. NCBI. Washington: National Academy of

Sciences, 2016. https://www.ncbi.nlm.nih.gov/books/ NBK384918/#sec_000020.

Clinton Foundation. "Engaging Community Leaders." Accessed March 1, 2021. https://www.clintonfoundation.org/our-work/clinton-health-matters-initiative/programs/ engaging-community-leaders.

Dispelling the Myths and Stigma of Mental Illness: The Surgeon General's Report on Mental Health. Issue brief. National Health Policy Forum, April 14, 2000. https://www.nhpf. org/library/issue-briefs/IB754_SGRptMental_4-14-00.pdf.

Facing Addiction in America: The Surgeon General's Report on Alcohol, Drugs, and Health. Washington: US Department of Health and Human Services, 2016. https://addiction. surgeongeneral.gov/sites/default/files/surgeon-generals-report.pdf.

Key Substance Use and Mental Health Indicators in the United States: Results from the 2019 National Survey on Drug Use and Health. Rockville: Substance Abuse and Mental Health Services Administration, 2020. https://www.samhsa.gov/ data/sites/default/files/reports/rpt29393/2019NSDUHF-FRPDFWHTML/2019NSDUHFFR1PDFW090120.pdf.

Lewinsky, Monica. "Shame and Survival." *Vanity Fair,* June 2014. https://www.vanityfair.com/style/society/2014/06/ monica-lewinsky-humiliation-culture.

The World Health Report 2001: Mental Health: New Understanding, New Hope. World Health Organization, 2001.